**A Little Humor Never Hurt Anyone**
Copyright © 2009 by Warren F. Hannas
ISBN-13   978-0-9822618-1-1
ISBN-10   0-9822618-1-0

Cover design by Amy Davidson
Book Block design by Amy Davidson
Front Cover Illustration by Jennifer Savage
All rights reserved. No part of this publication may
be reproduced or transmitted in any form or by any
means without written permission of the author.

# A Little Humor Never Hurt Anyone

WARREN F. HANNAS

# ABOUT THE COVER

When we're having a great time — lots of fun — we describe the moment as "having more fun than a barrel of monkeys!"

The monkey and emu on the cover, the "stars" of the picture, are two of my favorite characters of my stuffed animal collection. The monkey has been elected to be the delegate from the barrel of monkeys of which he is a member, and the emu volunteered to carry the monkey. The emu's legs are long, and he felt he could lift the monkey high enough off the ground to perpetually honor the monkey.

Just look at the emu; he has a big, broad smile on his face. You see — the happy face on the monkey and the emu's broad smile constantly remind us that A Little Humor Never Hurt Anyone!

# DEDICATION

THIS BOOK IS FILLED WITH HUMOR, HISTORY, and fun. all this characterizes the wonderful life my wife Julie and I have experienced together and shared over the past forty-two years. It is only fitting that I dedicate this book to Julie for all the humor we have shared, history we have lived, and fun that came along with all of it! Not only my wife, she's my best friend.

# ACKNOWLEDGEMENTS

One of the wonderful things I have learned in life is that where something good occurs, it rarely happens because of one person. This humor-intended chronicle is no exception. I am grateful to several people.

First of all, if it weren't for our granddaughter, Laura Ross Gabriel, and her history teacher, I would never have thought of this venture. Laura wrote me while she was in high school asking about two events in history. The teacher wanted the children to hear about history first hand. She asked about what life was like during the great depression and about the Chicago Worlds Fair of 1933. I got to thinking about several things in the past that might be fun to write about.

I thank my brother Allan for his valuable help in writing the chapter on his life with me.

In fact, I give him credit for rewriting it.

I thank Jean Elliott Lyon for her help in my writing about her father, Harold M. Elliott.

Charlie Wonderlic, CEO at Wonderlic, Inc. helped me present the chapter titled "Don't Call Me Sir" properly.

Mary Lee Allsbrook retyped a PDF file I had unwittingly ordered from Kinko's, so that the chapter on the World War II Retrospective would fall into place—pictures and all. This was a monstrous job that presented itself at the last minute!

Mary Lee's brother, "Big Dog" Jim Cochran, gave his time to help put the whole work in proper order.

My long-time friend, Jodi Bowman, accurately steered me to Jessa Sexton and O'More Publishing, who helped put the book in the wonderful form it is and helped me self publish, making the book a reality.

The most precious help I am so thankful for is my wife Julie's intricate editing of each of the manuscripts that comprise this endeavor. Not only did she help with punctuation, but also, if she didn't like the way a passage read, we rewrote the passage. The whole book reads better because of her help.

Aren't people wonderful? What would we do without them?!

# PREFACE

SOMETIMES BIOGRAPHIES ARE FUN TO READ. Sometimes they are very boring. Lots of things in my life have been very interesting, but if I were to just start out and chronologically describe my life this would probably end up in the waste basket —not that it won't anyway, but by sharing some of the memorable events in my life, it's just possible this might end up on someone's literary book shelf.

The book started when our youngest granddaughter, Laura, was in Parkland High School in Orefield, Pennsylvania. Her teacher asked the students to contact their grandparents to learn something about history first hand. Laura wrote us and asked specifically about the depression and about the Chicago Worlds fair of 1933, "A Century of Progress," as it was known. I responded to her with the two chapters that I kept and later used for this book. But her request got me started to think that there were other things in my life that were significant, memorable, and interesting. I had already written the "World War II Retrospective" to give to my kids, and I had brought "Dear Ajax" home with me from my Army service, so I had a good start on my literary odyssey.

History really unfolds in the "World War II Retrospective." Although it was written a few years after my return home from Europe, it never the less describes many of my experiences there, and it is illustrated with "V-Mail" drawings I sent home to my parents.

"Dear Ajax" was written at the end of each day as I sailed home from Marseilles, France, on the S.S. Exchange in December, 1945. In a way, it was a daily log of the journey from France to Newport News, Virginia, where we docked.

I'm guilty of telling something about my life, but I have lived a good life. I came from good parents; I had wonderful brothers, a caring aunt, and at the end you'll see I have a most wonderful wife. You should live so well!

Many of the things that occurred in my life had a good lesson. "Don't Call me Sir" taught me a very interesting principle for doing business. Some events are funny. "The Chili Cook-off" ought to tickle your funny bone, and "Philharmonia?—Yessir" put a college professor in his place. Some of these stories are just plain human. "Whatever Happened to Walter" is one of those. "Lovely Lilting Laura" is another. "Whatever Happened to Walter" is also somewhat historic, as is "The Chicago World's Fair." And there is controversy, too, in "The Race That No One Wins."

Although I'm prejudiced, I really think you'll find lots of fascinating events in A Little Humor Never Hurt Anyone. One of the main purposes of the book is to entertain you. "The Midnight Ride of the Royal Palm" is reminiscent of a notable train ride. It entertains me every time I read it—but then, it's a bit of history and happy memories for me, as the old Pullman trains may bring back happy memories to you, also. I sincerely hope the book will fulfill its goal for you.

Actually, this isn't my first venture into the world of writing books. Between about 1965 and 1980, I studied many things about people. The goal of the study was to capture, in writing, what we must do to become aware. Awareness was the big topic of the day back then. As it turned out, the study became focused on self-esteem. Self-esteem and awareness are virtually synonymous. The project culminated in my writing and publishing the book Be Somebody! A Practical Philosophy for All Times. I taught the concept in adult continuing education at Morton College in Cicero, Illinois, and at Lyons Township High School in La Grange, Illinois, my high school alma mater.

My life stories have developed ever since.

# TABLE OF CONTENTS

| 1  | What Ever Happened to Walter? | 19 |
| --- | --- | --- |
| 2  | The Chicago's World Fair | 23 |
| 3  | Meal Times Were Fun Times | 27 |
| 4  | Lovely, Lilting Laura! | 31 |
| 5  | Harold M. Elliott | 35 |
| 6  | A Hobby Ain't a Hobby 'Till You Share It | 41 |
| 7  | A World War II Retrospective | 45 |
| 8  | Dear Ajax | 111 |
| 9  | The Midnight Ride of the Royal Palm | 129 |
| 10 | Philharmonia?...Yessir! | 139 |
| 11 | My Entry into the Realm of Insurance | 143 |
| 12 | Leadership Turns Up Where It's Least Expected | 151 |
| 13 | Don't Call Me Sir, *%#@#&* It! | 155 |
| 14 | Here's a Discount for You | 161 |
| 15 | Weasel, My Love | 163 |
| 16 | The Chili Cook-off | 167 |
| 17 | Tolerance Came Easily, But Taught Hard Lessons | 171 |
| 18 | Frog Legs | 177 |
| 19 | Where'd This Kid Come From, Anyway? | 179 |
| 20 | Big Brother Ralston Raymond Hannas, Jr. | 185 |
| 21 | Allan | 189 |
| 22 | Aunt Harriet | 193 |
| 23 | At the End of the Meal: Dessert | 197 |

# ONE
## What Ever Happened to Walter?

THE DECADE OF THE NINETEEN twenties was a happy time in the history of our country—what a great time in history to open this book of stories! Many of the stories will have some sort of meaning to them, some will have historic significance, and we hope some will have a good measure of humor, too. All are meant to entertain you.

In those nineteen twenties, people seemed to have money to spend on whatever they wanted, and spending was at an all-time high. People went to shows, they bought new clothes, and they invested money in the stock market hoping to make more. In fact they hoped to reap a windfall! Buying "on margin" was a popular way to invest; you pay only a small portion of money to buy stocks. If the stock market went up in value, you could do quite well, but if the stocks went down, you had to come up with the remaining amount of money to buy the stock.

Many other people spent their money on bigger and better houses. But at the end of the decade—1929, to be exact—people began to think that maybe all this would come to an end. The trouble is, too many people thought the same thing at the same time, and when they went to sell their shares on the stock market, there were more sellers than there were buyers, so the value of the stock market went down, and it went down quickly. Furthermore, when the stocks tumbled in price, it caused the "Margin" buyers to come up with money they didn't have. It's described as the stock market crash of 1929.

So the market went down. So what? Today our stock market fluctuates way up one day, and way down the next. I can only surmise what happened, but here are some of the facts: people wanted to sell their stock, because they wanted to buy other things—such as homes—and send their kids to college. So when the stock market crashed, the value of their investments dwindled to almost nothing.

There was that other factor, though, that caused great panic. Too many people bought their investments "on margin," as we explained earlier. This is where many people got burned. They had to come up with the full price of the stock. Now, if they didn't have the money, it meant they had to sell their homes, their cars, which had just become a popular item among the people, and everything they had in order to meet their obligation.

Another effect was that no one could afford to buy homes and other types of real estate, so the value of real estate tumbled along with the stock market. All wanted to sell their real estate, but no one could buy.

Because people didn't have any money, and because businesses didn't have any money, workers lost their jobs; people could no longer pay mortgages on their homes.

Because they couldn't collect money people owed them, banks were forced to close; people who had savings accounts in the banks lost their savings accounts.

It wasn't an instantaneous thing for everybody. You see, the results of the 1929 panic lasted for many years. It was called "The Great Depression." It took a long time for the country to recover and to get back to the point where people could earn enough money to buy the things they needed.

Although my father kept his job, he nevertheless was forced to take a cut in pay, but we had enough money to pay the rent, and to keep food on the table.

It was in 1932. I was in second grade. One of my best friends was a really nice boy named Walter. Walter Neuske. He would come over to my house to play, and I would go over to his house to play. We had lots of fun together.

One day, Walter didn't come to school. That was strange, because Walter always came to school. At the time, I didn't think much of it, because anyone can get sick. But when Walter was out of school for about a week, I asked my mother what had happened to Walter.

Now, understand, I was eight years old, and my mother did her best to tell me that Walter's parents had "lost their home."

"Lost their home?" I asked. "How in the world could someone lose his home?"

"Do you understand that we are in the midst of the depression?" she asked.

"That's what everyone talks about," I replied. "What does that have to do with Walter's being sick?" I asked.

"Well," she began, "Walter isn't really sick. His parents could not pay to keep their home, so they had to move out. They could not make their payments to the bank, and the bank took the house. That's what happens when someone can't pay mortgage payments. His parents couldn't sell their home," she told me, "because no one had any money to buy it."

"Where did they move to?" I asked.

"No one knows," she told me.

"Will that happen to us?" I asked.

"We hope not," she said. "So far we have been very lucky, and your daddy still works hard every day."

"Golly, the depression is a really rotten thing when people have to 'lose their homes' and then just disappear."

To this day, I wonder where Walter is. I hope he's okay. I hope he's thriving. I'd really like to know.

# TWO

## The Chicago's World Fair
*1933-1934*

ONE OF THE MOST MEMORABLE EVENTS in the history of my life was the Chicago World's Fair, "A Century of Progress." It lasted over two years. The first year was 1933, and that was exciting. I was only nine years old. I think I got excited because my dad was excited. He looked forward to seeing the fair with such eager anticipation, that his enthusiasm penetrated every bone in my body. I wanted to go, too. I had just one problem: I had a hernia. Now, in those days, the best they could do for a hernia was to operate, and then keep the patient in the hospital for about three weeks, and then have the patient spend the next six weeks at home in bed — most of the time — recuperating. So I didn't get to see the fair until late in the summer. I tell you: I just couldn't wait to see the fair! At least when I went, I was healthy.

And I did enjoy the fair. We walked from one end of it to the other. There were exhibits from many other countries. As I think back now, I can still remember the exhibit from Belgium. They had their very famous statue in the midst of a very attractive brick circle. Do you really want to know the name of that statue? Okay.

It was called "Manniken Pis." It was made by a Belgian king whose small son became lost one day. He sent his soldiers out to search for the little boy. Thinking the child would be found dead, the king said to his soldiers, "I want you to tell me the exact position my boy was in when you found him." The boy was found quite alive: taking a leak in the creek! The pose was immortalized. True story!

I remember the Sky Ride, and how we rode from one side of the fair to the other. The Sky Ride consisted of a tower on the west side of the lagoon and a tower on the east side of the lagoon. Between the two towers a cable car type system transported people to the other. The Sky Ride was one of the symbols of the fair. It was the big drawing card!

Aaah, but for me, the most exciting exhibit was the transportation building. I have been a train lover all my life, and 1933 was no exception. It was awe inspiring to see trains that had come from all over the country—new trains, from railroads I hadn't even heard of at that time. Back then I didn't realize the historical importance of the Transportation Exhibit. The first streamlined train was there: the Union Pacific M10000, a pretty three car train, brown on the top and bottom, and yellow in the middle. The Burlington Zephyr was there, too. It was the first streamlined train with a diesel motor. The Zephyr was a glistening, silver, three-car train with a slanting nose that just looked as though it could speed anywhere! The Milwaukee Road's "bi polar" electric locomotive was there. In those days, "bi polar" did not mean a locomotive with depression! That locomotive was huge and pulled heavy loads in the Cascade Mountains of the northwest.

The highlight of the exposition was the pageant in the evening called "Wheels A-Rolling." It was the story of transportation from the Indian sleds, to the beginning of trains, and up to the end of transportation at that time. The finale was even more exciting! Read on.

But 1934 was the exciting year for me. It was in May that the Burlington Route had just presented its new train to the world. It was America's first diesel "streamliner." They wanted to show what the train could do, so the Burlington Railroad ran the new "Zephyr" named after the God of the West Wind, Zephyrus, from Denver to Chicago, and they did it all in one day!

We all stood beside the track in the little town of Western Springs, Illinois, where I grew up, and waited for the train to come through. It was late afternoon when we looked westward toward Hinsdale and saw the tiny headlight appear. It grew and grew until on the middle track, the fast track, this sleek, shovel-nosed, glistening, three-car phenomenon sped by so quickly that if you had blinked your eyes, you'd have missed it! It traveled from Denver to Chicago—1016 miles—in just 13 hours and 25 minutes! And where did it stop? That night it was the finale on Chicago's lakefront at the World's Fair's "Wheels-A-Rolling" pageant! It remained the pageant's final act until the end of the Fair. To most people, the event might have been insignificant, but to a 10-year-old train loving boy, that was a big deal! And, by the way, you can see that awesome three-car Zephyr today on display at Chicago's Museum of Science and

Industry.

Today, it's almost as if the age of the once glamorous streamliners never existed! Although the Zephyrs grew in size, they now have never the less disappeared, and Amtrak has claimed the rails. Those days of the beautiful trains were magnificent—an unforgettable period of time!

And so was the A Century of Progress, the Chicago World's Fair of 1933!

# THREE

## Meal Times Were Fun Times

My brothers and I were pretty lucky kids! We grew up at just the right time. Even in my youth, I would think of the kids that grew up just 50 or 100 years before me. Their dads went to work at dawn and didn't come home until after dark. They hardly saw their dads! Yes, my brothers and I were lucky!

As I look back, some of the happiest times we all shared as a family was dinner every evening. My dad was editor of a magazine called The American Poultry Journal. Usually he was home, but once in a while he had to travel to a college or a university to tune in on some sort of research that was designed to help the poultry industry. Or maybe he had to attend a convention somewhere that had to do with better ways of raising chickens, turkeys, or ducks.

When he came home, he was full of interesting stories that he would tell us about those trips.

We always heard about the filet mignons he had at this hotel or that, or the lobster that was the most succulent he had ever tasted. Mother used to sit there and stew because she never got to be included in those exotic meals dad described. She wished he could have put them in a to-go box, I think, and brought them home to the family.

Mother was a good cook on Sunday. She was a home economist, too, self taught, or taught by her mother, I'm not sure. But it was economical to have a nice roast—beef, lamb, or whatever—for Sunday dinner and then have leftovers the rest of the week. Mashed potatoes usually went with the roast, and then we had mashed potato cakes the rest of the week. So you see, it was no mystery as to why dad always dreamed of the steak, lobster, and all the other goodies he used to describe.

But the meals were always healthful, even though they lacked imagination. The fun came among all three of us boys. All of us seemed to like trains—yeah, even mom liked trains. Her father had been a civil engineer with the Pennsylvania Railroad until he died. We used to play word games and guess initials—not just any initials, but railroad initials. Now all of us knew the regular, popular, well-traveled roads, but every now and then, after he returned from one of his trips, dad would come up with an initial we weren't familiar with. Oh, I'll tell you he felt right pleased about stumping us with something like the B & A. "Is it Baltimore and 'Ahio,'" we'd ask?

"No," he would say. "Try again." Finally, when he saw he had us completely stumped, he'd tell us of a freight car he had seen from the Bangor and Aroostock. He explained it's a railroad that serves New England and was probably based in Maine (which it was). So not only did we learn railroad initials, but also we learned geography!

We also learned our state capitols that way. We'd give one another the name of a state, and the one directed the question would give the answer — if he knew it! Dad would say, "Warren, what's Tennessee? I think I usually came up with Nashville. We learned a lot eating dinner, and I'll tell you, mealtimes were fun while we were growing up!

But sometimes we had to learn other things at dinner — like manners. I don't know why, but mother's sister, our Aunt Harriet, always sat next to me at the dinner table. Conversation was going along well, until all of a sudden, I'd feel a tapping on my elbows, which were probably supporting my head. Aunt Harriet, in a very quiet voice that was heard all around the table, would say, "Elbows off the table, Honey Dear." Gosh, why did I have such a hard time remembering that?

Dad had a tremendous sense of humor. He almost always had a good joke or two for us. I guess when one travels a lot and comes in contact with other people, one of the greatest communication devices is always humor. Now it wasn't just jokes he'd tell, which were usually good quality humor; however, Dad was a punster. We all used to like performances by Bennet Cerf, an acclaimed author and editor.

But by far the greatest benefit of mealtimes was learning what each of us did during any given day. As I have already said, Dad told us of his day, but Mom was busy, too. She would tell us of her adventures with her lady friends at church circle, D.A.R. (Daughters of the American Revolution), and whom she met while shopping. When mother shopped, she met several friends, and what she learned from them she shared with the family, and we knew what was going on around town.

The meal times we shared were certainly the basis for our meal times while Julie, my wife, and I raised our family. We insisted on everyone being home for dinner so we knew what our daughters were doing all day long. Meal times should be fun times for everybody!

# FOUR
## Lovely, Lilting Laura!

GRADE SCHOOL, ELEMENTARY SCHOOL—call it what you will, it's absorption school. Here's why: we learn reading, writing, and arithmetic, a smattering of social studies, some drama, art and—if we're lucky—music. Ahhhh, music!

I was never a star pupil in any of the subjects I took in grade school. I learned to read early on, and that stuck consciously with me forever. I learned composition, but writing didn't congeal until I was in high school. I learned arithmetic, but that didn't come into focus until I was in college! I did okay in social studies, and I was just slightly better than average in art—well, drawing, anyway. And then there was music. Music. What a sleeper! Today classical music is a very important part of my life.

My appreciation for classical music began in fourth or fifth grade. The school superintendent, Dr. Leonard B. Wheat, felt quite happy about his accomplishment of installing a public address system in all of the rooms of McClure School in Western Springs. Every afternoon at about 2:00 o'clock, over the loudspeakers came a program from New York! It was a music appreciation program featuring Dr. Wallter Damraush. He pointed out many fascinating facets about classical music selections, about the make-up of the symphony orchestra, and sometimes even about a specific instrument. For some reason or other, I took to this program. I liked it; I can't recall it changed my life at that point, but I absorbed it.

My next memory of music in school was in junior high school, seventh and eighth grade.

We had a teacher named Miss Raguse (pronounced: Rag' u ZAY'), Laura Raguse who also taught art. I always liked Miss Raguse. One of her projects was what she called the Special Chorus. I was chosen to sing in the Special Chorus. I really didn't have a very good singing voice, but I guess I could sing second soprano. We sang at school functions, and we always put on special programs at Christmas and Easter.

We sang the usual Christmas songs, but she introduced us to many we had never heard of: "Indulce Jubilo," "Jesu Bambino," and it was the first time I had heard the traditional "Oh Holy Night." It's now one of my favorite Christmas hymns. She directed us so that we sounded really good, no doubt better than most seventh and eighth graders. One time, Miss Raguse took us down to the Merchandise Mart in Chicago to record some songs to be played on Chicago radio station WMAQ. Exciting!

It's strange; you know? Some how or other, I never pondered about the songs we sang then, but now after being out of school for many years, I hear a concert with some of the most prominent stars like Luciano Pavarotti, Placido Domingo, and others, and they perform those "different" songs Miss Raguse taught us back in seventh and eighth grade. Today, I look back so fondly upon Miss Raguse and upon that music—the music I learned about from New York on the loud speakers during fourth grade, and the "new" songs Miss Raguse taught us in seventh and eighth. The phenomenon is that although all that music didn't mean much to me in those school days, I absorbed that musical training and appreciation. It's all an important part of my life, today. Thanks, Miss Laura, one of my favorite teachers!

# FIVE

## Harold M. Elliott
*(4/25/1903—3/25/1967)*

OTHER THAN THE MEMBERS OF MY immediate family, one man stands out in my life as one of the most important and influential people I have ever known. He had a very successful business, he had a good family, he was a religious man, and he had a dream. Now, at this point in his life, I was aware that he had one daughter in her teens, but he also had a very young son. He nevertheless spent a great deal of time helping other young men form their lives in a most positive way.

I was a sophomore in high school when I first met Mr. Elliott. In those days, we didn't address our elders by the first name. He was Mr. Elliott. One night Dick Williams, my best friend, and I thought we'd look into the Hi-Y club as part of our high school activities. We drove to the First Presbyterian Church of La Grange, walked in the front door, and timidly descended the creaky wooden stairs to the basement. As I remember, there was somewhat of a labyrinth of pale green wooden walls that led us to where a small group of our school chums and upperclassmen were finding seats on the metal folding chairs.

Soon, this imposing gentleman, who was six feet three inches tall with thinning hair, walked into the room. He greeted the fellows he knew and shortly began the meeting. It was Mr. Elliott. We opened with prayer and with the pledge to the American Flag; every week there was a religious devotional program, and we closed with prayer. That's about all I can remember about that meeting. Why the prayer? Why the devotions? We were the Hi-Y Club, the high school club of the YMCA. We didn't even have a Y in La Grange in those days. The YMCA was reputed to be a Christian organization. That's what the "C" stands for: Young Men's Christian Association. My pal Dick Williams and I were impressed, and we joined the club.

As time went on, it became clear that Mr. Elliott was devoted to the idea of starting a YMCA in La Grange. He had a dream. We often asked about this YMCA. "Will it have a pool and a gym?" we prodded, "and can people sleep there?"

"It will have all of those things and a whole lot more," he would tell us.

Now I was familiar with the YMCA because my dad had given me a membership in the Central YMCA on La Salle Street in downtown Chicago. Every Saturday during that time, I rode the train into Chicago and walked over to the Y, where I enjoyed swimming, some gymnasium work, and fascinating field trips we almost always went on. So I was familiar with the YMCA. I'll tell you—the prospect of having a Y like that in La Grange was dynamic and exciting!

Now I sit here writing this, trying to remember what we did and what we accomplished at our meetings. I can remember that we often had programs—movies, for example—but we gelled as a group; we developed fond friendships and grew up remembering the friendships we had made there.

We occasionally went on field trips, too, and twice a year we went out to the forest preserve south of town for picnic suppers. I can remember having the usual fun: like baseball, touch football, and other physical activities.

For me, the big thing was the campfire we always had. Devotions around the campfire were both impressive and meaningful. Mr. Elliott's favorite hymn was "I Walk in the Garden." We all sang that hymn frequently. To this day, it's one of my favorites, too. Toward the end of the picnic supper, we would form a large circle. At that stage in my life, I wasn't at all good at making prayers, and I guess maybe there weren't very many who were, so, going around the circle, each of us gave very short testimonials, "one liners," statements of thankfulness, perhaps.

When the proceedings had finished, there was one thing left to do: that was to put out the fire. You may think this is strange, but Mr. Elliott had to show us how to put the fire out—as only boys can do very effectively.

Well, time passed. When I graduated from high school, I went to college, which was interrupted when I was drafted into the Armed Forces. I returned to college and graduated from Purdue University in February 1950. I had no touch with happenings in La Grange, or in the life of Mr. Elliott.

Although I didn't know about what was happening, Mr. Elliott was working with other successful businessmen in town, raising money to build that YMCA. Did they succeed? You bet they did! The West Suburban YMCA opened its doors with an attractive, well-equipped gymnasium, an Olympic-size swimming pool, comfortable, hotel-type sleeping rooms for people who needed a place to stay, and meeting rooms for organizations for both men and women. The Y even had handball courts! And when I returned, instead of Hi-Y, I became a member of the service club of the Y, Y's Men International. And that's a subject for another story of my life.

Harold Elliott's dream had come true! He had planted the seed, he had nurtured its development, and he actively served on the board of directors until he died in March 1967. That Y should have been named the Harold M. Elliott YMCA.

Then, one day there was a movement to change the name of the Y. There was a man named Rich Port who had successfully built a large real estate empire in La Grange. He, too, contributed many hours, and loads of money to the Y. Rich Port made a multimillion dollar deal with the West Suburban YMCA. One of the conditions was that the Y be named the Rich Port YMCA. Now, although I served on the board of directors of the Y, I didn't like the deal, but the Y did need the money badly. How I wanted to name that Y "The Harold M. Elliott YMCA." I nevertheless voted for naming it the Rich Port YMCA—but I didn't like it. The big deal went through anyway.

Although the Y is named for Rich Port, I shall always be blessed with my memories of Harold M. Elliott, and I am blessed with the religious support from that Hi-Y club. In my mind Mr. Elliott will always be a part of my life. May God eternally bless you, dreamer, actuator, doer, and volunteer, Mr. Harold M. Elliott!

# SIX

## A Hobby Ain't a Hobby 'Till You Share It

I CAN REMEMBER THAT WHEN I was a small boy my dad had a rather extensive stamp collection. I think of stamp collecting as a rather introverted type of hobby. It gives somebody something to do when no one else is around.

However, Dad's approach was remarkably different. Sunday afternoon was his time to put up the card table in the living room. Then he got the stamp albums from his study, and he brought out the stamps he had acquired and put the new stamps into the album. I could probably barely see over the top of the card table when he went to work on his hobby. I was fascinated by those tiny little stamps. Some were small and square; some were bigger and oblong shaped. And—gosh—there were some that were triangles!

Dad would pick up the stamps with a pair of tweezers and hold them so I could clearly see them. "This is from a country called Switzerland," he would explain. "See that mountain? It's in the Alps, and it says, 'Helvetia.' And that means Switzerland. The Alps are in Switzerland."

"What about those triangles?" I would ask.

"Those are from Africa," he'd reply, and he'd tell me a little about Africa. I learned a lot from Dad's stamps.

The important thing is Dad shared his hobby with me, and with my two brothers, too. Just imagine how much geography we learned from Dad's stamp collection! In fact, my older brother collected stamps, and when Dad passed away, my brother, R Square (see chapter 20), inherited Dad's collection. But I just know Dad's sharing his hobby with us enhanced the collection for him while the knowledge he gave us enriched our lives.

Today, my hobby is trains: big trains, little trains, passenger trains, freight trains, real trains, train pictures, all kinds of trains—even trains from around the world! Today my hobby is vibrant and active, a wonderful part of my life.

It wasn't always like that.

When I married my first wife, I was young, and she accepted my fascination with trains as part of my life, but she figured that as I aged chronologically, I should also "grow up." As the Bible says in the Gospel of Matthew, I should leave my childish ways behind me. So my trains went into boxes. My fascination for trains wouldn't die, though. After all, trains had been with me practically since I was born. But part of me was in "squelch-exile." That first marriage ended after 14 years of hoping things would turn around.

Three years after the first marriage closed out, I remarried. It wasn't long until my new wife, Julie, learned I had some trains in boxes. I had built them when I was in high school and in college from scratch.

They were made to scale from tin cans, cardboard, and pieces of wood.

"What are they doing in boxes?" she asked.

"Well," I replied, "my first wife made me grow up and put my trains away."

"They aren't doing any good in boxes," she said," Why don't you get them out so all of us can enjoy them?" Oh Boy! My friends, there was hobby enrichment! I soon started buying and selling model trains, and the proceeds financed my participating in and expanding my wonderful hobby of model railroading. Through my enterprise I became quite conversant in matters of all types and all gauges of model trains.

Ultimately when the Nashville science museum, known as the Adventure Science Center, generously displayed a very attractive "O" gauge model railroad, I was appointed chief engineer, and I directed the running of the trains there for about 20 years.

Today I am active in several railroad clubs including a full-blown railroad museum. My Julie participates with me, and most of the things I do I share with her. At this writing, I have been married to my very wonderful wife for more than 40 years. She participates in my hobby with me, and I participate in her hobby with her.

When she was younger, she had a hobby, too. She repaired dolls. And believe it or not, I did participate in her hobby. If repair was needed to a part of a doll's body, I was able to use fiberglass, cardboard, super glue, or whatever it took to mend the doll. I was the "body man." Together, although we fixed the doll, we nevertheless found one very important truth: we really restored a woman's roots. With her baby doll looking like new, the customer really had an important part of her life restored. We enhanced the lives of many people. We have helped to interest folks in model railroading, and we have helped rekindle fond memories for many women and their daughters. And beyond that, you know, my working with Julie and her dolls and her helping me and my train has enhanced our marriage beyond all manner of comprehension!

I tell you, folks—a hobby just ain't a hobby until you share it!

# SEVEN

## A World War II
*Retrospective*

BEFORE WE START...

This might be a bit different from the usual war story. You see; I was in heavy field artillery. Our guns were the mighty 155 guns, sometimes referred to as rifles because of the long tubes. We called them long toms. Our guns were free standing. Long toward the end of the war, the army began mounting these guns on tank chassis, which made them easier to set. In one of our locations, we were plagued with mud; the self-propelled guns would be easier to handle in that situation.

But by the nature of our materiel (guns, etc.), we spent most of our time well behind the established front lines. What made the environment even safer, I was in fire direction center of the headquarters battery, 200th Field Artillery Battalion, 190th F. A. Group, Fifth Corps (most of the time), First Army, under General Omar Bradley. As such, I saw almost no face-to-face action with the enemy. So what you'll be reading about is my history during World War II—from beginning to end. My life consisted of many anecdotes, and that's the way the war was for me. I do hope you'll enjoy reading about World War II from a somewhat different perspective.

The illustrations that begin later in the story were drawn on "V mail" paper. A "V Mail" page was not quite as large as an 8 ½ X 11 sheet, but it was close. It was printed in red ink. The object of the "V Mail" was to write a one-page message which would be sent to a "V Mail" center somewhere in Europe. At the mail center, the pages would be photographed onto micro-film. When there was a full roll of film, the roll was shipped to a V Mail center in the US. There it was transcribed—developed—and printed onto a page which was about 4" X 6". So, the recipient of the "V Mail" actually received a black and white photograph of the original page. Most of the time a picture came through clear and legible, but sometimes they were over-exposed or under-exposed.

Instead of writing letters on these "V Mail" forms, I drew pictures, and those pictures are what you see later. There were a few more pictures that aren't printed here because they were lost in a fire in our home in 1995.

Enjoy!

## Part I

*Introduction*

I HADN'T YET FINISHED MY FIRST YEAR IN COLLEGE when a letter came to my home, it read something like Your neighbors have selected you to serve in the armed forces of the United States of America. That made sense. After all, most of my neighbors had daughters, and I never particularly got on well with them anyway.

So, on the 9th of July 1943, I met with a fairly good-sized group of my high school classmates and several others at the city hall in La Grange, Illinois. After hearing official encouraging words, we walked in formation to the Burlington train station, where we boarded the morning local for Chicago.

In Chicago, we were met by an army person who marched us over to a building not far from Union Station. We went up three or four floors to where we all were given physical examinations.

Found to be in good physical condition—I was able to see lightning and hear thunder—I was asked which branch of the service I wanted to serve in. I chose the army. Before long we were whisked back to Union Station where we boarded a special train for Camp Grant, Illinois. It was both glee and with apprehension that gripped me as we sped through La Grange and Western Springs, my old, home stompin' grounds, wondering when I'd see them again.

Now, there's one rather fascinating detail I ought to cover here. In the group of us that was inducted that day, I had a friend with whom I had attended high school. His name was Warren Goodlad. Warren was a year behind me, actually, but we were rather good friends anyway. Warren and I rode together to Camp Grant, where we were separated by assignment. This isn't the last we'll hear about Warren Goodlad.

Camp Grant must have been a rather good place because my recollection of events there is somewhat scant. I do remember that Camp Grant was a sprawling collection of barracks lined up row upon row upon row. How would I ever know where I was to stay? I certainly can't recall the building to which I was assigned, but I do know it wasn't until after they had given us new clothing that we found out where we'd be staying.

I remember the clothing issue very well. They asked my sizes, and where I knew them, I told them, and I was tossed the underwear, shirts, and trousers I was to care for as if they were my very own. At the end of the line came the shoes. "What's your shoes size, soldier?"

"Ten," I replied.

"We haven't got a ten, soldier. Take these. If they're too uncomfortable, bring 'em back; we'll do what we can." Now the reason I remember this so well is that all the years of my life, I had gone to shoe stores to buy my shoes, and the store clerk always measured my feet to get the proper shoes for me. It so happened the shoe size the army man gave me was size 10 ½ - B. It was the most comfortable pair of shoes I had ever worn! Ever since then, I have known my shoe size to be 10 ½ - B. I knew the army had to be good for something!

During the time we were at Camp Grant, we marked identification on all of our clothing and learned how to pack the duffle bag. There was an art to that; believe me.

After we got all of our clothing, we were issued our mess kit. It consisted of an oval pan about nine inches on the long part of the oval and about eight inches across. It was about two inches deep. The cover to the pan part was like a vegetable dish divided in half. They were made of sturdy aluminum, and held together by two rings. The handle of the mess kit folded into the under side of the divided vegetable dish, which became the top of the mess kit. A sturdy knife, fork, and spoon were included, fitting snugly into the pan of the kit. Anyway, it was simple, utilitarian, and a great companion to have with us always!

However, this was a kit with no written instructions. In fact, we weren't even told how to make a mess with it. These were our eating utensils. Every time we reported for mess—mealtime—we would have our food served into our mess kit. Now mealtime—mess—was always a fun time. It was always what we called the "chow line." We went to the mess hall to chow down. Sometimes those serving the chow would be friendly as they placed the food into the mess kit, but more often than not, they'd throw a serving spoon full of mashed potatoes, vegetables, meat, and whatever at the mess kit, just hoping they'd hit it. They'd always ask, "Where would you like it?" We'd point to the place, and then they'd throw it wherever they felt. "Don't worry," they'd tell us. "It all goes to same place, anyway." It always got a chuckle. The mess kit would be ours until the day we mustered out—except in my case. Upon separation from the military I asked to keep it as a souvenir, and they let me do it. I guess they figured that the initials "W.F.H." artistically etched on the pan of the mess kit really wouldn't fit in the U.S. Army.

The next day we reported to the parade ground for drill. Now, I had had a year of R O T C at Purdue University, so they asked me to drill the rest of the troops in my group. I don't remember what we called the group, but we were all to be assigned somewhere into army service. The one thing we knew is that we would be known as replacement troops.

Daily we were tested and grilled, and drilled and fed. Finally, notices began to be posted telling when we would "ship out." My friend, Warren, shipped out one day, and I wasn't assigned to go with him. However, one week later, my day came, and I enthusiastically boarded the troop train. Now we weren't told where we were going or what we were going to do, but since I was assigned to a Pullman sleeper, I knew I was going some distance away.

In the morning our train left Camp Grant. We went over Milwaukee Road tracks from Davis Junction, to Chicago, and all the way through Union Station. We stopped in the coach yard of the Pennsylvania Railroad, about a mile south of the station on the east side of the main line tracks. Finally, in the middle of the afternoon, we left and traveled eastward over the Pennsylvania Railroad. We really sped. Knowing much about railroad lore, I knew how to clock the speed of the train, and we flew down the pike at 88 miles an hour! We stopped at Fort Wayne for a crew change, and then on we sped.

The next morning, we went through Washington Terminal, through the tunnel, and on toward Richmond, Virginia. We still kept going. The Virginia countryside was heavy pine timber country and was beautiful to behold.

Night came, and we reached our destination, which, for the first time, we learned was Fort Bragg, North Carolina.

WARREN HANNAS

## Part I, I

*Basic Training*

WE MARCHED TO A MESS HALL — remember, that's army talk for a dining room. I never quite knew why the dining rooms were called mess halls. The truth is, they were really quite clean, and the "mess" — the meals — were really quite good! I don't know how I was so lucky, but throughout my Army career. I always got good cooks.

Anyway, after we ate dinner, we were marched to our barracks. The barracks were all the same — row upon row of them. The floor plan was the same, and one barracks was just the same as the next, and none of them were stylishly decorated with drapes, carpets, or the niceties of suburban living. The barracks at Camp Grant had green roofs, and the barracks at Fort Bragg had red roofs.

No, instead, the floors were bare wood, and there were two rows of beds downstairs, and two rows of beds upstairs. The rows of beds were arranged so that the foot of the beds were on the aisle. At the foot of each bed was a chest for keeping items of clothing, etc., that didn't need to be hung up. At the other end of the bed — the head of the bed — was a locker for the things that needed hanging. Lavatory and toilet facilities were at the end of the building, on the first floor. This area was known as the Latrine, pronounced La Treen'. Directly over the lavatory was the barracks leader's quarters.

Anyway, by the time we were assigned to our beds, it was quite late. The consideration the Army gave us was that we were allowed to sleep late the next morning.

When morning came, and everyone else had been summoned out, we were being awakened for breakfast. At break-time, the other troops paraded through our barracks looking for familiar faces. Would you believe! I was greeted by my friend, Warren Goodlad. He was, indeed, a happy sight! Warren and I were destined to enjoy many happy times during our weeks in basic training at Fort Bragg, NC.

Basic training for me was quite interesting. I had been assigned to what was called "Instrument and Survey." Now, the Army was pretty good at naming things in a practical way, so you can understand exactly what I learned. Our day started with reveille, breakfast, and then classes. In the afternoon, we had calisthenics and drill. After supper was our free time, which meant we could even go into town if wanted to. Fayetteville, North Carolina, was not far, and the Army Post ran regular bus schedules into town and back for us.

Reveille was always an inspiration—using the term somewhat loosely. Every morning reveille occurred as a bugle rendition. It's sad I can't sing it for you in prose. You had to hear it to know what it was. However, it's a bugle call familiar to anyone who has ever gone camping in any kind of group. The barracks sergeant would walk up and down the aisles making sure everyone awakened. Sometimes his message was, "Okay, guys, drop your cocks and grab your socks!" We got up, washed, and all that, and got ready for breakfast—mess.

Then the sergeant stood outside the barracks building shouting at the top of his lungs: "All right men fallout! ...Faster!...I want to see some casualties falling out of that building!" When we were properly assembled, we had to "dress right," which means we extended our right arm to touch the shoulder of the man next to us, and turn the head to the right. That being accomplished, we stood inspection, hearing almost everything that was wrong with us on that morning. Inspection out of the way, we paraded to the mess hall for breakfast.

Army training included a lot of things that didn't necessarily have to do with where we would ultimately be assigned. For example, each of us had to help in the kitchen. It was called being assigned to "K.P." which stands for Kitchen Police. Our jobs on K.P. always were to do the horrible things that none of the cooks or dining personnel cared to do. One of the most horrible tasks was to clean the grease traps. K.P. is usually characterized by someone sitting over a huge vat peeling potatoes, and that was also a part of the day's assignment. K.P. lasted from about 4:00 AM, when we were awakened, until about 7:00 or 8:00 PM when our duties were finished. Fortunately, it was only one day at a time.

Another non-curriculum duty to which we were often assigned was "policing the area." This was usually a platoon or barracks' assignment. We were marched to an area that needed to be cleaned up, and then set forth to pick up off the ground every scrap of paper, every cigarette butt, and any other kind of debris which we could grasp. The commands for this were always very amusing. "All right, Men," we were addressed, "don't leave anything lying there unless you can' t pick it up!" Or more often, "All right, men lean over and start picking everything up! I want to see nothing but ass holes and elbows working this ground!" We were all inspired to really get to work. "Policing the area" was an activity in which we would engage many times during our military careers.

Another activity that we would always have with us was guard duty. No basic training would be complete without guard duty. We were handed a list of 10 general orders—or was it 12? —and were told to memorize the list. We were frequently quizzed on those general orders, as it was quite necessary that we know what to do and how to do it while on sentry duty for whatever we would guard during our careers.

Guard duty was really not bad. As was the case with everything else, we learned of our assignment from the bulletin board outside the squadron headquarters (our row of barracks). We were assigned a 24-hour period where we had 2 hours of actual duty and 4 hours off. When it was our turn to serve, we were awakened by a representative of the Officer of the Day—the "OD." We were assigned a territory to guard, and we walked the assignment with rifle on the shoulder, ready to use it if the need arose, which it really never did. The biggest hazard was the "OD" himself coming around to quiz us on our knowledge of the 10 or 12 general orders. We had to stay on our post until we were relieved. Like K.P. and all the other extracurricular assignments, guard duty was meted out quite fairly.

In our classes, we learned how to direct fire for the cannons that were always remotely placed from us, and we learned how to survey. We learned about metro messages, or weather sampling, because climactic conditions had an effect on the trajectory of the ammunition, or rounds, we fired.

The atmosphere in which we worked was very loose and democratic in the class periods. It was all discipline, of course, on the drill field. Being an entrepreneur, I bought cartons of candy bars at the Post Exchange, commonly called the "P X." During our breaks, I stored the candy cartons on the shelf in the locker by the head of my bed. I sold the candy bars to my fellow trainees, and I made enough money to buy a very nice little personal radio. It was a really nice little unit, typical of good Motorola quality.

Things went well for quite a while, until one day we were told we were going on bivouac. I looked forward to that eagerly. It meant going into the "outback" of Fort Bragg, camping, and staging maneuvers out there. One day while we were out maneuvering, away from the camp, a fire got started, and it burned up all of our possessions. We lost our tents, our clothing, everything—including my dear little Motorola radio. Of course, the only thing Army replaced were the Army or "GI" equipment. ("GI" stands for Government Issue.)

I continued to sell candy bars to my fellow trainees, and after a short while built up a very good volume of business. But all things must come to an end, and indeed, the candy store was no exception. One fine day, I felt so badly when I awoke, that I found it necessary to go on "sick call." Sick call was usually the stomping grounds for the "goldbricks." It seems the doctors got to know who the lazy ones were, and they treated them in their own inimitable way. When the doctor came to me, he didn't recognize me. Alas, I was not one of his regulars. To me, it seemed like he was taking an awful lot of time to take care of me and my ailment, whatever it might be.

Finally, I was directed to sit on the other side of the room. A truck drove up outside, and I was really beginning to feel badly. I was weak, and all I wanted to do was to lie down. I knew that if only I could lie down I'd feel better. The doctor came in with the truck driver and pointed to me and said to the man, "This is the one I want you to take."

So I was ushered out of the sick bay and into the waiting truck that turned out to be the ambulance. For some reason or other, I didn't feel quite so weak anymore, and I was allowed to sit for the ride to the Post Hospital.

The Post Hospital was my home for the next six weeks to recover from a rather severe case of pneumonia. I really made some good friends there among the medics—the floor personnel. When I recovered from the illness, I went back to the barracks. Everything I owned was still in its place where I had left it. Only the candy bars had been removed.

I was sent home on a two weeks recovery furlough. As I left, I said good-bye to friend, Warren Goodlad, and wished him well in his assignment wherever it might be, and of course he wished me the same. It was nice to be home and to see all my friends and to take things easy for a while. When I went back to the base, I resumed my basic training. The group I had started with had graduated.

I really had only a few weeks to go until I finished. On one or two occasions, I was able to visit with the hospital corps medics who had been so cheerful in treating me at the hospital and I made a few new friends, who I knew would be very temporary. And when the final day of my basic training came, I again got a furlough, this time to report back to Fort George G. Meade, Maryland.

For me, it meant a couple of really great train rides and a good chance to see our Nation's capitol. I spent only a couple of hours of a couple of days seeing the city, but I did enjoy what I saw.

When I reported to Fort Meade, I was assigned to a barracks, and it wasn't long until I was informed that this was a holding place for troops who are assigned to go over-seas. While strolling from one place to another, whom should I spot but good old Warren Goodlad! Now, Warren had shipped out of Fort Bragg on schedule after completing his training, but after he arrived at Fort Meade, he too had contracted pneumonia. So, between his furlough time, and mine, he was still a week ahead of me. And sure enough, one week after he left for who knows where, I too shipped out.

## Part I, II
*Crossing the Atlantic*

EVERYDAY, WE INSPECTED THE BULLETIN BOARD by our row of barracks to see who was on the shipping list. When my name appeared, it told me where to report, duffle bag packed, ready to travel. All we knew was that we were shipping out. We never knew where we were going, or when we'd get there. But we were always philosophical about it. After all, we had all the time in the world, and there was no way we were going to muster out—not with a war going on.

So we showed up where we were supposed to on the train's loading platform, and climbed aboard. This time, it was day coaches, so I knew I wasn't going far. You see, every move we made, we tried to out-guess the Army, but it never did any good. Another army characteristic was that we report at 9:00 in the morning so that we could start our journey by noon or ever later. We knew it as "hurry up and wait." It was always best to keep an open mind, which we did, and we always found ourselves where we might least expect.

In this case the train pulled out of Fort Meade and onto the Pennsylvania Railroad 's main line. We headed north, and went through Havre de Grace, Philadelphia, Princeton, and Trenton. Now, this took place in March 1944. I don't remember inclement weather at Fort Meade, but as we traveled north, the outdoor temperatures began to drop. Our train slowed on the outskirts of New Brunswick, New Jersey, the city where I had been born. I had an aunt who lived there, and since the train drew to a stop, which turned out to be lengthy, I wanted to get off the train and call her. Ah, but no way, Jose, after all, I was in the midst of a secret troop movement! Reality struck again.

It was late at night when the train finally resumed its journey, and the next day we found ourselves in a bleak, cold, snowy camp, and we got off the train and walked to the barracks where we were assigned. What do you know! The same bare bones decorating scheme all the other barracks had.

After a while, we found that the name of the Camp was Miles Standish. We were in the Boston, Massachusetts, area obviously preparing to cross the Atlantic. Well, let's say it didn't make any sense to gather here for shipment to the South Seas. We spent much time indoors because this was not the time to frolic outside. Man, I mean it was cold! We weren't at Camp Miles Standish very long until our names appeared on the shipping list. When our names were listed, we reported trackside for train boarding again. This was not to be a long trip, but it was to be fascinating. We left the camp in the afternoon, and arrived in Boston in darkness. Our train inched its way through yard tracks in Boston's industrial section and came to rest beside a huge pier. Just across the platform was a really good-sized ship! It was comforting to know we would at least have a large ship for the ocean crossing. We walked up the gangplank and were directed to the area where we would sleep.

What ship is it? We all wanted to know, but as they say, "Nobody knew nuttin'." We were assigned to a place about two decks below the main deck. I'll tell you: these ships were fixed up to carry people by the scads! For example, there were posts from floor to ceiling. Around each post were four cots…four cots five high. In other words, there were 20 sleeping cots on each post. I have no idea how many troops were aboard, but there were a lot!

We must have been the last troops to board, because after we bedded down for the night, we felt the engines start, and we could sense motion.

The next day we went up on deck. We were allowed to do that as long as no emergencies arose. When we got up on deck, we saw we were one of six ships sailing together. One of the ships was obviously the sister ship to ship we were on, and there were four others. Circling all around us at all times were destroyers. Sometimes there were two, and sometimes there were more. We were also accompanied by dolphins frolicking beside and among the ships.

One day a storm came up, and we were all ordered below deck. The ship began to roll a bit, but since we knew what was happening, we really didn't worry—well, most of us didn't worry. All of a sudden there was a WHAM! CRASH! as the ship shuttered and shook. Four men ran up the stairs as fast as they could. They were sure we had been torpedoed. But alas, we had simply been struck by a gigantic wave that struck us broadside. It had hit so hard it smashed one of the life rafts to smithereens.

On another day, I was walking in the chow line getting close to where we went below for the mess hall, when whom should I spot, but my medic friends from the hospital. We enjoyed a short reunion, reminisced a bit, and hoped we'd see each other again—but it never happened.

From time to time, we were able to shower. The shower was right off of the latrine. And where would one find a latrine? The Men's room? Forget that noise, Charlie; both were in the swimming pool! It was the most incredible plumbing I had ever seen. There were long sewer pipes stretched along the floor of the pool, with commodes sitting on top of the pipes at intervals of just a few feet. Okay, all you folks who want privacy, stand up! Get off the ship!

As our voyage proceeded, we were able to spot little things that began to identify our ship. It soon became apparent that we were sailing aboard the Moore-MacCormick Line's luxury liner, SS Argentina. The sister in our convoy was the Uruguay. In peacetime, these liners sailed between New York City and South America. Many years after I had been home from the service I purchased a beautiful painting of the SS Argentina at a Garage sale. It hangs in my den, today.

On the tenth day, we got up, and wow! The ship had really calmed down. The water was incredibly smooth. When we walked up on deck, we found we were in an estuary rimmed on both sides with beautiful, green, gentle rolling hills. Well, it wasn't long before we learned we were in Scotland. Hey, where's our tour guide; why didn't she tell us? Anyway, the journey up this "Firth" was slow and drawn out. How nice. Soon we stopped, and small boats came out to unload the ship. I don't know where the other ships were; as I remember, our ship was all alone. Anyway, we were transported into a very small town on the shore. Its name was Greenock, pronounced Gren' ock. As I remember, we boarded the train right from the pier. Shortly, the train left the station and went into a long tunnel. It seemed we were in that tunnel for a long, long time. But when we emerged, we looked out the window, and lo! There was our ship out in the river, and below was the town we had just left! The tracks had gone through the tunnel, circled around, and came out over the city. What a gorgeous sight lay before us!

The train proceeded through Glascow and Edinburgh and headed south through a rather desolate part of England. I can still hear the wheels of the train characteristically singing, "Da-da-da-da, da-da-da-da." It was rhythmical and seemed to say, "Son of a gun, Son of a gun." It was different from our American trains whose song was, "Da-da-da.....da-da-da" (those big old six wheeled Pullman trucks). Well, excuse my love of trains, but that's the way it was.

Along the way, we stopped at a station somewhere, and ladies came out with coffee and pastries. Wow! That was neat.

Again, we arrived at our destination in the middle of the night—usual destination: "Who knows?" We rode to the camp and were assigned our accommodations. I ended up this time in an upper bunk. No sweat. I could sleep anywhere in those days. Now, since we had arrived late at night, we were again allowed to sleep late in the morning. The first thing I recall, someone pulled the blanket up off of me. I rolled my head off to the side of the bunk to look down, and when I did, I saw two very familiar eyes looking at me. It was Warren Goodlad! My ol' buddy from home! Warren! He had arrived last week.

## Part I, III
*The Eto: European Theater of Operation*

THE FIRST ORDER OF THE DAY WAS to find out where we were. Everyone seemed to know we were in Heath Camp, Cardiff, Wales. Everyone, that is, except me, until I asked.

Training in this camp became exercises of great fun, as I recall. Part of the reason for this is that we took long hikes—excuse me, marches. We marched out into the Welsh country side, which was unique. There were gently rolling hills with farms of fascinating composure. Rows seemed to be round, and even spiral-like. Many of the farms and fields made the countryside look like a huge quilt. It was really beautiful.

At this point, we were regarded replacement troops—men who would be assigned to military units which, by the time we reached them, would have sustained casualties. Our camp was known as a replacement depot. The name replacement depot was always shortened to "Reple Depot," depot pronounced with a short e. Our home will forever after be known as the reple depot.

Our accommodations at Heath Camp were not bad. They were small wooden huts, which were warmed with stoves. They were comfortable. One interesting thing was that daylight lasted until 9:00 PM or later. It was known as "Double B-r-r-ritish Summah Time," daylight savings on top of daylight savings time.

Writing home was not always easy. We didn't know what we could or could not say to our folks. Usually, we just wrote what was on our minds, and the army censor would cut out—literally—what he didn't think should go through the mail. Secrecy was extremely important. One of the ways I communicated with my parents and friends was with the "V-Mail." This was a single piece of paper, approximately 8 ½ by 11 inches printed in red. The top two inches was marked for the addressee and the sender, and rest of the page was for the message. According to the instructions printed on the back of the V-Mail, we simply wrote our message, folded it, and mailed it. The government then took a micro film picture of it, made rolls of film, and sent the film to the United States.

When it got to America, each microfilm was printed onto a small piece of photographic paper and sent to the addressee. It saved a lot of bulk shipping across the ocean. You will see several V-Mail drawings I made for my parents. They were thrilled with them and saved them for me until I eventually got home. In fact, you have already seen two of them on previous pages portraying the British (Welsh) countryside.

While at Heath Camp, we drilled and we marched and we stood guard duty. Nighttime was something else. By this time, all of England was under siege from the Nazi Luftwaffe, which meant that many nights, the German air force came over and bombed the living daylights out of England. Wales, being adjacent (I guess the word should be contiguous.) to England qualified it for frequent bombing. Man, I tell you—I don't know a more woeful and startling sound than that air raid siren. It started at a very low pitch and worked up to a high, raucous frenzy, maintained the wail for several seconds and then lowered back to nothing, only to begin again.

During the air raids, we were led out to trenches to wait until the all clear rang. Sometimes we could see action, and other times we couldn't. All during the air raids, the searchlights combed the sky looking for the German planes. Once in a while we could see one get caught, and when the light spotted it, it got shot at, and usually plucked out of the sky. Many times, since we could see no action, we could sleep in the trenches. I'll tell you, though, we woke up fast when the bombs hit near us—Crang! Bang! Whang! they'd go. Air raids were not fun things to be in.

Heath Camp was within walking distance of Cardiff.

Cardiff, Wales, was an interesting place. In the center of town is Carnervon Castle. I have always been fascinated by castles, and Warren and I walked all around the building, but it wasn't open to the public.

In Cardiff, we got our first introduction to Fish and Chips. In those days it was distinctly British, and for me it was a real treat. I really loved those fish and chips. The British "chips" were what we call French fries—Mmmmm—Good!

It was also our first introduction to the British people. What a disillusionment! These people resented our being there! Can you imagine that? They outright told us they wished we'd go home. I really didn't need that, as I would gladly have gone home, but I thought we were there to save the British. Alas, we were their allies, not their friends. All around the city, we would see barrage balloons. I suppose they were designed to keep the "Jerry" planes high, or at least be some kind of an obstacle for them. We kinda figured they were there to keep the British Isles from sinking. As we would say today, "Oh well." After about a month, we were all transferred to another camp southeast of Wales. Near the town of Yeovil, England, was Camp Houndstone. This was a nice camp, and Yeovil was a nice little town. As in Heath Camp, we did a lot of military drilling and marching. I seem to recall having leisure here, though, as we stayed in large Army tents. All of our facilities were out of doors.

Everyone knows what a latrine is, and what it is used for, but what do you do in a small shelter named "ablution?" Ah yes, it was here I leaned a new word. These were the little open huts where we washed, and to wash was to ablute. Do you suppose we could also have laved?

I guess I should describe here that our uniform consisted of the dark green clothes known as "fatigues." They were comfortable clothes with long trousers and big side pockets. We had also been issued steel helmets. Under the helmets, we wore the plastic helmet liners. These were also rather comfortable, and the fatigues and helmet liners were the usual dress of the day. The helmets were designed, so they told us, for everything from washbasins to toilets when we got into battle.

I remember once I took a short walk, where I saw some wild flowers. I picked up a dandelion, and put it in the little hole on the front of my helmet liner. As I returned, I was standing by the gate when a jeep drove up with army folk in it. One of the people was a captain, and he saluted me. I saluted back, of course. But the jeep stopped, and backed up to me, and the captain asked, "What's your rank, soldier?"

"I'm a private, sir," I replied

"Get that dandelion out of your helmet, soldier! NOW! You look like you're trying to impersonate a major!"

Great day in the morning! The last thing I would want to do would be to impersonate any officer. That's a serious offense. Needless to say, I complied post haste!

It was at Houndstone that I learned about Haystack Annie. Haystack Annie was a prostitute. She peddled her service outside the camp anywhere there was something to hide behind. No, I never availed myself of her services, but it was amusing to see a line of guys—not really in a line, but lined up many, many feet apart so as not to be conspicuous, waiting their turn for "Annie." After all, I had a sweet lil' gal back home I was waiting for. (Okay, so you have heard that before! In my case it was really true.)

Warren Goodlad and I had many nice times together at Houndstone and in Yeovil, but we were to split up very soon, as you'll see.

I had guard duty several times at Houndstone, so it seemed to me, but I really didn't mind it. One night, guard duty was fascinating, disruptive, and insightful. All during my watch, plane after plane after plane went overhead, flying low, and pulling gliders—two to a plane. A good sentinel keeps his mind on the area he's guarding, which I'm sure I did—would I admit to anything else? But nobody needed to draw me any pictures as to what was going on—the invasion was starting, and I was seeing it before it happened! Wave after wave of aircraft flew over as I walked my beat that night.

Of course, the next day was no news to me, but the effect was that we were put on alert, and a couple of days later we shipped out of Houndstone. Our destination at that time was a small camp near the coast of England. We stayed about a day and loaded up after dark onto a small yacht. During the night we crossed the English Channel. When the sun came up, we could see we were one of what looked like a hundred boats! We transferred from the yacht to a smaller boat—a landing craft.

We approached the beach of France. Now, this was a destination they told us about. It was known as Omaha Dog Red Beach. The sand of the beach came closer and closer, and we were admonished to keep low, until soon the boat stopped. The end of the boat lowered, and we simply ran off the front of it, and onto the beach.

"Keep low, and take care of yourselves!" they told as we disembarked.

Once on the beach, we were marshaled in a small area, where those into whose care we were entrusted led us. We marched about 5 miles inland, to a densely wooded area.

The French landscape was even more interesting than the Welsh country had been. We marched through a small town, passing small houses made of stucco and rock. Farms were separated by dykes and gullies. They called them hedgerows. It was early June—D-Day plus six, to be exact—and France was really very green and pretty.

It wasn't long before we reached the forest where we were to bed down. During the daytime it was quite beautiful, but at night it was hair-raising! Just as we settled down to go to sleep, we started hearing guns fire, and up in the air the whoosh of the shells passing over head was startling, and I must say, somewhat dismaying. The sergeant in charge came down the path and made sure every one of us was pushed down into the long trench to protect us. After all, they told us, we were only about 200 yards behind the front line!

This was also my first experience with K-rations—breakfast in a box, lunch in a box, and dinner in a box. Hey, listen; it could have been a heck of a lot worse! We had a small can of beans or a meat-type "entrée" along with some crackers and cheese. The whole thing fit into a small box about 9 inches long, 3 inches wide, and about 2 inches thick.

We spent two nights there, and on the third day, a truck came to pick some of us up. My name was called, and I gathered up my duffle bag and clamored onto the truck. I was anxious to get out of there! There were only about ten of us to go, and we all sat on the benches waiting for the truck to start. Soon we were rolling, and the truck took us to the unit we would be assigned to, into battle officially. We drove to a point 8 miles behind the lines! It was here I found my "outfit," the 200th Field Artillery Battalion, part of the 190th Field Artillery Group, assigned to the First Army, Fifth Corps.

## Part I, IV
*The 200ᵗʰ Field Artillery Battilion*

IT WAS A BEAUTIFUL SUNNY DAY AS OUR TRUCK—our 6 by 6 as they were called—drove into the field where we were to unload. A 6 by 6 truck got its name because it had six wheels: a front pair and a tandem axle behind, and all six wheels were powered. "6 X 6" is how we described them.

Upon our arrival, we were given a friendly welcome by one of the officers, and then, as our names were read, we followed to where we were assigned. I was assigned to Headquarters Battery.

Along with one other man, we were led to a big tent where Headquarters Battery Commanding Officer, Captain Horace Hall, welcomed us. The first day involved digging a foxhole alongside one of the ubiquitous hedgerows. We encamped there with our tent halves, our duffle bags, and all of our worldly possessions.

I feel badly that I can't remember the name of the man I shared the tent with, but we got along well and reported regularly when we were supposed to report for duty. We were assigned to fire direction center in Headquarters Battery of the 200th FA Bn.

The heartening revelation of the day was that the 200th was a battalion of long toms—155 millimeter rifles. These guns were something else; let me tell you! They had a maximum firing range of about 16 miles. That's the distance from La Grange, Illinois, to downtown Chicago, or from Franklin, Tennessee, to downtown Nashville! It's effective range, however, was about 8 miles. That means the guns could fire accurately to a target 8 miles away. It also meant that our distance from the front line was anywhere from 2 to 6 miles behind the front lines, at any given time.

The 200th Field Artillery Battalion used to be the 2nd battalion of the 190th Field Artillery Regiment. It was designated the 200th FA Bn on November 1, 1943, while stationed at Great Torrington, Devon, England, (A) . The 200th FA Bn was part of the Pennsylvania National

Guard, with representative cities being Du Bois, Sunbury, Punxsutawney, Clearfield, and New Castle. Headquarters Battery was from Du Bois. Many people from other places had joined the battalion before it left the United States, however. The battalion sailed for England on August 31, 1942, aboard the HMS Queen Elizabeth, arriving in Greenock, Scotland, September 6, 1942. (B).

During the first couple of days in the new assignment, many funny things happened. Probably the one with the most pathos involved my tent-mate and me. Oh, I wish I could remember his name! He said to me one morning as we awakened, "Gee, I'd sure love to have a drink of fresh milk." Now, as we looked from our tent, we could see a herd of cows, and on this one morning, there was an elderly lady tending the herd, so I suggested we ask the lady if she'd give my friend a drink of milk.

155mm LongTom
200th Field Artillery Battalion

---

(A) Taken from: 200TH FIELD ARTILLERY BATTALION, The battalion's history, written and published, Pilsen, Czechoslovakia, 1945.

(B) IBID

We studied the English-French translation manual we had been given and found the words to ask for some milk. Slowly, the two of us approached the woman, and, with open book, uttered, "Doh nay mwah du lay." (Donet mol du lait.)

We never knew whether the woman was really happy to see these two Americans or frightened out of her wits, but she handed over all the milk she had! We couldn't make her understand we only wanted a little bit. So we had a full day's supply of milk.

Fire Direction Center was in a separate tent. Two large tables were pushed together, and on top were battle area maps furnished by Army intelligence, I guess. They were very accurate maps of the territory into which our huge long toms fired. Three of us sat alongside the table in folding chairs with an army slide rule and a telephone. The man in charge of the tent was a captain, and there were three of them, one for each "shift." A picture of our Fire Direction Center is on the next page. When I made this drawing, we had received some enemy artillery shells into our area, so we all took cover. I believe that is Lieutenant Thompson reporting to Corps headquarters.

The man in charge over the Fire Direction Center was our "S-3," a Major Carl Wolfe. I generally worked under a Captain Gordon W. Van Hoose, a Shreveport, Louisiana, plantation owner. He was a delightful man with a good intellect, and a good sense of humor along with a very stern sense of discipline. In the "FDC" when the telephone rang, a forward observer was on the other end of the phone, telling where a target was.

"FIRE MISSION!" Captain Van Hoose shouted.

We all rang up our telephones to the battery each of us was assigned to work with. As I remember, I was assigned to Battery B most of the time. At the other end of the telephone was the person in charge of telling the cannoneers how to aim the guns.

As the captain gave us the range and the angle of the target, we computed the settings to instruct the gun battery. The captain would say, "Range: 8,000 feet. Shell, HE. Charge 5. Left 250 degrees."

The guns had their own aiming posts set up, so we would translate the commands to be "Charge 5. Elevation 35. Azimuth 210." Our slide rules computed how high to aim the guns for whatever the range was. The range, of course, was the distance from the guns to the target. The azimuth told the cannoneer how far to the right or to the left to point the gun. The ammunition to the guns came in three sections. One was the projectile. Another was the casing—the shell, you might say. The third was seven bags of gun powder that could be cut apart, depending upon the size of the charge. Charge 5 meant that 5 of the seven bags of gunpowder went into the casing that would power the projectile. Then there were different types of projectiles. They were referred to as "shells." There were High Explosive (HE), Armor Piercing (AP), smoke, and others.

When all the commands had been relayed to the gun batteries—there were three: A, B, and C—then the command was given "FIRE!" and bal-loom! Nine guns gave the enemy real trouble.

When the guns set up, they were hauled into place by the prime mover, which I'll describe shortly. The towing wheels were removed, and the gun trails were spread. Exactly how they did that, I never knew because I really never saw them set up. But I do know that when they had the gun in position, one of the cannoneers set out a stake in front and to one side of the gun.

Next, they set their azimuth reading to "0." Then they would move the gun according to the commands we gave them. One of the reasons why the guns were so accurate was that they were relatively easy to adjust.

Azimuth and elevation settings were accomplished by rotating wheels with perpendicular handles. The handles turned shafts that were geared, and the geared shafts drove the gun to the proper height or direction.

The alphabet that the Army used was a universal military alphabet. The letters, of course, were A to Z, just like any alphabet, except that every letter had a name. It made it easy to understand every letter, and mistakes in communications were thereby kept to a minimum. The alphabet started out Able, Baker, Charlie, Dog, Easy, Fox, George, etc. So when a letter application arose, the name of the subject was the name of the letter. That means that although I was in Headquarters Battery, I was computer for Baker Battery. Able and Charlie Batteries had their computers too.

The gun batteries were located about the countryside somewhere. The distance between our Fire Direction Center (FDC) and batteries ranged anywhere from ½ to two miles. You can see the task the telephone linemen had every time we set up! Our telephones operated on a "Simplex" system whereby part of the current went by wire, the other part through the ground.

We went all across Europe that way with one fire mission after another. We supported infantry troops, usually, which meant our targets were out in front of the foot soldiers, and we were to try to get the enemy to retreat, or at least hide so that when our troops got there, the target was easy to capture. Well, that was the goal anyway. Hey, listen; it often worked, too!

Sometimes we were given "T.O.T." missions — Time on Target. We were told to have the guns ready to fire at 0630 hours, which meant 6:30 AM. Perhaps there would be an offensive timed for early morning to take the enemy off guard. At 6:30, our guns were fired, and the battle was under way!

Sometimes we were given "interdiction" missions. These were where we aimed guns at particular road crossings. It might have been learned through intelligence that Germans were moving over a certain road during the night, so we would fire rounds of ammunition to certain crossroad with great irregularity. They would know the rounds were coming in, but they'd never know when — like "waiting for the other shoe to drop."

Our battalion supported troops in the battle of St. Lo; we helped close the Argenton-Falaise gap, which trapped hundreds of Nazi troops, and we went on from there, to Paris, with several skirmishes in between.

When our work was done at an installation, we were given the command: "Close Station. March Order!" When this command was given, we gathered up all the maps and slide rules and packed them neatly into the huge wooden crates, struck the tent, and packed it onto our trucks. We, in headquarters battery traveled mostly in the standard Army 6 X 6 covered by a removable canvas. If the weather was clement, the canvas was partially uncovered so we could get some nice sunshine.

The guns were another story. You see the drawing I made of the gun and its prime mover. Just over the trail of the gun, which means just behind it, you can see a pair of wheels. These became the trailing wheels and were attached to the guns trails, and they were hooked up to a "trailer hitch" in back of the prime mover. The

155MM Gun M1 and Prime Mover

prime mover was mounted on the chassis of a General Sherman tank, but instead of a tank body, a cabin was made for the driver and behind him, the cannoneers. Goods were often carried on top of the vehicle.

The battery entourage usually consisted of some jeeps in front carrying the commanding officer of the battery, reconnaissance personnel, and other officers. 6 X 6 trucks with other battery paraphernalia such as the battery kitchen, and other service facilities, and then the guns followed by maintenance personnel in a jeep.

Our headquarters battery had no guns, but we had other things that required mostly jeeps, personnel carriers, and 6 X 6s. The personnel carriers were larger passenger vehicles that defied description, but suffice it to say, they carried a driver and four or five other passengers and were mounted on high axles.

Most of our moves were made in the daytime when we didn't need lights. Our aircraft pretty well ruled the skies by this point in time, so air attacks weren't very

---

1( C ) 200th FIELD ARTILLERY BATTALION, a history of the battalion written and published in Pilsen, Czechoslovakia.

frequent. Our vehicles had little tiny lights for night movement, though, which looked like cat eyes.

Now while we were not in actual combat situations, we always operated on the basis of 50 minutes on and 10 minutes rest. That means while we traveled from one installation to the next, we would ride for 50 minutes, and rest for 10. One of the early rides was somewhat frustrating for me.

The French people loved us! Everywhere we went, they were there to welcome and to watch us. They threw us flowers, tomatoes, and homegrown goodies—they'd throw them to us and at us! But they stood beside the road cheering us on.

Well, mostly when we stopped, we utilized the resting time to care for the homespun little tasks Mother Nature required us to handle. Once, our convoy drew to a stop in a highway cut. The French people—mostly women, mind you, because most of the men had been used in combat somewhere—stood on top of the rise over the roadway and gazed at us. Now, at this point, my bladder was full almost to overflowing. To a very modest, shy, sheltered suburban boy, this was a dilemma. What was I going to do?

One of the seasoned soldiers, seeing my problem, came over to comfort me. "Hey, " he said with a wry smile. "Don't worry about it. Just do it! If they've seen it before, they know what it is. If they haven't seen it before, they won't know what's happening." Ahhh. I felt better already! I guess you call it growing into the realities of life: my first public pee.

On or about the 24th of June, we pulled into a very nice hillside location, where all of us dug foxholes for safety. We usually selected a site near the hedgerows. A friend of mine, Louis Viviani, dug his foxhole (What else could you call them? Manholes are parts of sewer system!) beside a bush in an opening in this field. The kitchen crew had set up higher up the hill across from my foxhole, and about 20 feet across from Louis'. It was almost noon on the 25th of June (C) when Louis decided to go up to the mess tent a little early for lunch. As he reached the kitchen we heard the tell-tale screech of an artillery round coming in at the close of our European mission. "BAM!" Right in our midst the shell exploded. Where did it hit? It was a direct hit on Louis Viviani's foxhole! Had he waited just a moment or two to get out of his foxhole, he'd have been killed! The grace of God was with him that morning, or as we used to say, "His number just wasn't on that shell."

The next day, some of us walked back into the woods next to the encampment. We wanted to see where that round of ammunition could have come from. We think we saw the source of the shot.

Not very far into the woods, we came upon a small Nazi tank. It was grey and camouflaged and had obviously been captured. Whether it was fired by a Nazi or an American no one could tell, but there it sat for all of us to inspect. The V-Mail drawing came out rather dark, but there it is on the next page.

*[V-Mail illustration captioned "Captured German Mark VI Tank and Yank Inspectors"]*

We had a very wonderful First Sergeant named Loyce Robertson who hailed from Gadsden, Alabama. He had been with the outfit for some time and had been through the days in England, including training with the 190th FA Battalion on the moors of England. According to the men in the battalion, those training days were somewhat rugged.

Well, one day, in the middle of August in 1944, we pulled into position near a little French town called Vire. A private named Paul had been drinking very heavily. We had come from the section of France called Calvados. Calvados is a liqueur known for its distinct potency, an aperitif named for the Province. Paul had been drinking plenty of Calvados, and I suspect some cognac, too. The man was so drunk that he could hardly stand up. Now, he was a communications man, and he wasn't doing his job. 1st Sergeant Robertson approached Pvt Paul to ask him to give up the bottle of liqueur, but Paul refused. The 1st Sergeant pleaded with Paul to give up the bottle, and finally ordered Paul to relinquish it. "Please give me that bottle, Paul," Sergeant Robertson repeated.

"You gitcher hands off my bottle or I'll kill you," Paul said. But Sergeant Robertson pulled on the bottle, and Paul shot the wonderful first sergeant point blank. The sergeant slumped to the ground, and several men came running over when they heard the shot. Paul was put in irons, taken away and later tried in a court martial, where he was convicted and sentenced to die by hanging.

In one of the fields where we camped, we often heard the most woeful cry of some animal not far away. When I was off duty one time, I pushed my way through the hedgerows to see what was making that strange noise. To my surprise, it was a donkey braying to beat the band. I just wanted to try my hand at portrait work, so there is my result on the next page:

> His funny looks amuse me ever
> And I laugh when I see him
> Dance.
> I know I'll not forget the invasion
> Nor that little donkey back in
> France.
>
> He's contented when he's eating
> And also while someone is near
> Him;
> But leave him alone and shoot a
> Gun,
> Then you can clearly hear him:
>
> eee-ee-ee-ee-
> HAW !!
>
> My First Work In Portrait Art (?)
> V--MAIL

In late August, we reached the outskirts of Paris, in a suburb called Herbouvillier. We weren't there long, because Paris had been declared an open city. This meant both sides agreed not to fire on the city in order to save it.

It also meant that the next day we drove through the middle of Paris, past the Bois du Boulogne, onto the Champs Elysee, in a parade where the French people went wild to welcome us! Wow, it was great to have friends, and the folks in Paris were sick of the Germans; let me tell you! It's one of the best parades I have ever ridden in. After the parade, we drove to Noisy Le Sec, another Parisian suburb, where we stayed for several days.

## Part II
*Paris, the City of Light*

You know, I have been holding out on you: I have really only talked about three batteries in the 200th Field Artillery Battalion. Actually, there are four. The fourth battery is the service battery. It has charge of procurement and maintenance. That goes for everything from the food we eat, to the vehicles we drive, to the maintenance of the guns.

Thanks to our service battery, we took a ten-day rest in Noisy Le Sec. As we mentioned in the last chapter, it is a quiet little suburb on the outskirts of Paris. We were there to get our tubes changed. After the guns had fired a certain number of rounds (shells), the tubes were worn to such a point that the guns no longer fired accurately. The tube of a gun was a hardened steel insert within the barrel of the gun, which had the spiral lands and grooves needed to give the shell a spiral twist as it is fired. The shell traveled through the air much more accurately with that twist, thereby enhancing the control of the fired round or shot, or shell.

Well, by the time we reached Paris, these hardened steel inserts, the tubes, had worn to the point that they had to be changed. So service battery arranged, with the Ordnance section of the U.S. Army, to come out to perform the action. The process would take about ten days.

My goodness! What will all these troops do while

the guns are being serviced? I'll tell you what they'll do; they'll go see the sights of Paris! Indeed, what a break! What a great vacation!

Now before I start talking about our time in the city, let me tell you a little bit about Paris and its people at that time. For the most part, the French were ecstatic that the Germans had been driven out. They wee equally delighted that the city had been declared "open" to protect it from damage.

The economy was somewhat unstable, so special currency had been issued. The French Franc—the unit of currency—had been issued especially for those days by the allies, and the Americans had issued special dollar bills. Where silver certificates seal was blue, and the Federal Reserve note was green, the allied Expeditionary Forces currency had a yellow seal. All the currency was good, legal tender and used for normal transactions. But, alas, there was another unauthorized, though acceptable, "currency" the French preferred. It was the American cigarette. Ah yes, one cigarette got lots of goods, and a carton—WOW!—a carton of cigarettes was like gold! Since I was a non-smoker, I felt like the Bank of America!

My personal needs were small. I stopped at a street vender's cart that had post cards for sale, and I picked out about 25 post cards and some large-sized cards of places like the Eiffel Tower and Nortre Dame Cathedral. How much? Just one cigarette would do.

I had heard much about the Paris Metro—the subway system—rated one of the best in the world. The French, and the Parisians in particular, were so happy to have the American come to the city, that we rode free.

Being a train fan, I rode from one end of the line to the other on all of the lines.

I took full advantage of the city in all aspects. The American Red Cross had set up a bureau in the city, where we could borrow bicycles. I rode all over town! I saw the Eiffel Tower and walked up to the first level. At that time it wasn't open above that. I rode around L'Etoille, the Arc de Triumph, down the Champs Elysee, through the Place de la Concorde, past the Louvre, up the Rue de la Paix, home of Chanel Perfumes, around by the Place de L'Opera, and up to the Sacred Heart, a beautiful glistening white cathedral high on a hill overlooking the city. Gosh, I wonder what that kind of a tour would cost today. On a bicycle, I felt as though I were part of the city, because almost everyone rode bikes

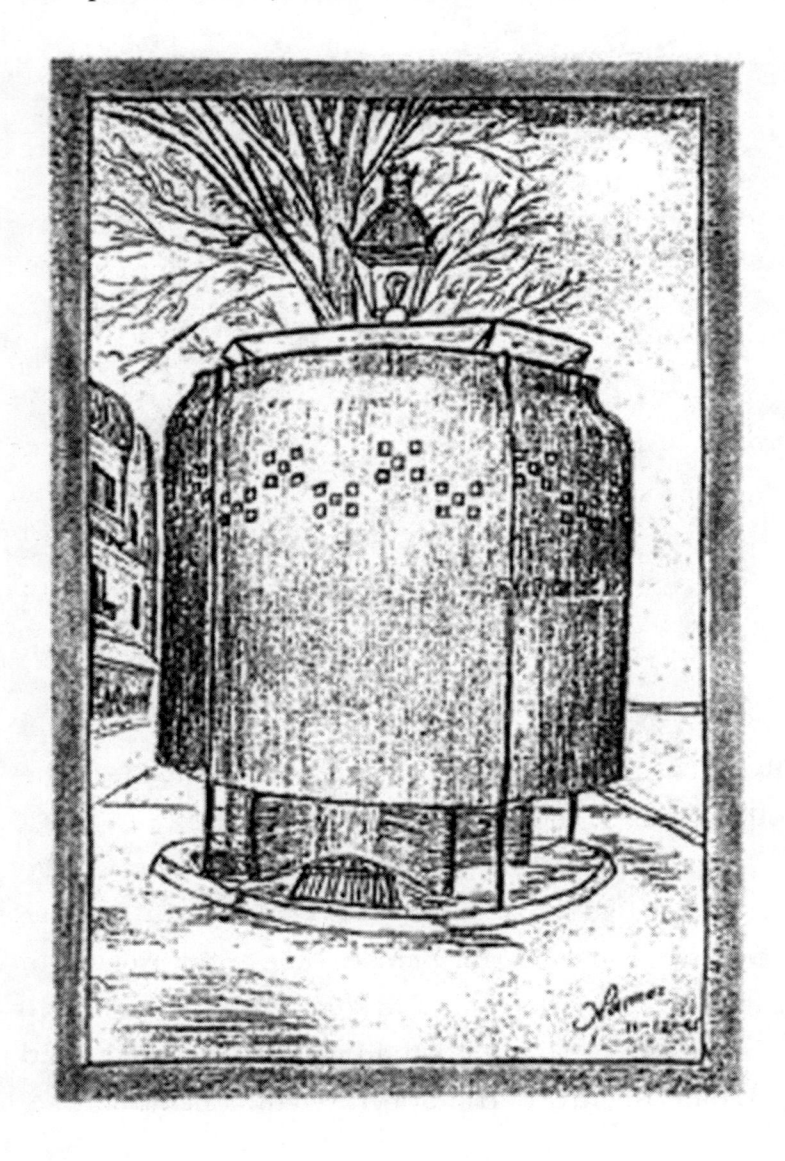

then. Gasoline wasn't readily available to everybody just yet. Oh, and everybody loved the Yanks!

I also did a lot of walking in Paris. It was fun to stroll on the Champs Elysee from L' Etoille, the Arc de Triumph, down to the Place de la Concorde. In English, Concord Square had an obelisk commemorating The Bastille. Along "Champs" were places for men to relieve themselves. Descriptively named, L' Pissoire, it was common to see the ankles spread wide while a man was taking a leak. It wasn't discriminatory; a woman could go there if she wanted to, but I never saw it happen. The Europeans are far more tolerant of nature than we are in America. By the way, the message printed on the structure was "Defense D'Afficher"—No Advertising.

Another thing I often encountered on my walks around the city were venders selling roasted chestnuts from the carts. You can see the pan at the end of the cart with a small sterno type stove beneath it and bags of chestnuts ready to roast. Note that the soldier wears the "A" of the First Army. That is what I wore on my sleeve.

Paris held yet another fascinating escapade for me. It was the first time I had attended grand opera. Paris had, and I presume it still has, two opera houses. One was the primary opera house, "L'Opera," and the other was the "Opera Comique." The Opera Comique staged light opera or comic opera, whereas L'Opera featured classical or grand opera and others, too. When I attended the performance at L'Opera, Le Roi Dys was on stage. The King of Ys, written by Edouard Lalo, is an opera worth seeing on any stage, but the French have an unusual talent for dramatic effects. Near the end of the opera, a tower exploded in a most dramatic way! I loved it, and I have liked grand opera ever since.

We were driven into the city by one of the drivers of our battery, and we met the driver when it was time to go back. The ten-day interlude in Paris was one of the most delightful periods of time during the whole war. All too soon, Ordnance finished its job on our twelve guns, and it was time to resume the war.

# Part III

*Journey to the Rhine*

Well, with wonderful memories of Paris to cherish, the time had come to load up and move out. It was September 2nd as our convoy assembled. Our commanding officer, Col. Andrew W. Roth, saw the "parade" was in order and mounted up in his jeep at the head of the line. Then came our battery commander Captain Horace Half. A supply truck followed, and then the truck I rode in. It was known as a 6 X 6, which meant it had six wheels, and all six wheels were powered. The rear of the truck was covered like a covered wagon, and we all rode on benches inside the cover. The benches were attached to the side of the truck. Behind us were more supplies, and then batteries A, B, and C followed with their leaders, their personnel, their newly outfitted guns. and their supplies. Quite an entourage.

Our destination that first day out was a small town 60 miles away in the vicinity of Attichy. Our actual bivouac was called Vic Sur Aisne (Pronounced: Ain), where we stayed for about four days. While we were there, townspeople walked up and down past us and brought us tomatoes and other goodies to eat. Many folks just wanted to chat with us. They probably wanted to try out their English skills. We were a real attraction to them! I tell you; the French people were so glad to see us!

Let me say at this point that I'll quote dates and maybe name some places and possibly other things no man could conceivably remember. My primary resource is a book published at the end of the war (no date given) titled 200th Field Artillery Battalion. No author is named. I presume every member of the battalion got one. Anyway, it is a very accurate, detailed account of practically every move the battalion made from deployment to England on the Queen Mary to the end of the war. However, my memories are strictly mine.

We crossed from France into Belgium on September 10th. The town was Libramount. Here we saw how the Belgian people treated the women who collaborated with the Germans. They paraded the women naked through the streets with their heads shorn to completely disgrace them. The war was surely over for them! Or was it just beginning?

On September 12 we went into Luxembourg. We were really getting to be world travelers! The next day the battalion set up just 3600 yards from the German border, and we fired our first rounds (shots) into Germany 2 days after that. 3600 yards is just a little over 2 miles. For us, that was close, but when we were in pursuit of the enemy we set up close, and then it wasn't long before the enemy had retreated such that we ended up perhaps 16 to 17 miles away. Our target was the Siegfried Line at Brandscheid Germany.

On October 3rd we moved into position at a small town called Butgenbach (pronounced Butch' en bok). Some of my most vivid memories of the war were in Butchenbach. Our headquarters battery was set up in a schoolhouse, but we slept in a home nearby with a family. I'm not totally clear about this, but I believe the family lived elsewhere while we occupied their home. I do remember that it was the first time I had slept under a featherbed mattress. Whoo Boy! You talk about comfort; this was sheer luxury!

Now the boy who lived in the house was named Joe—at least that was what he called himself. He claimed to be about 14 or 15 years old. He listened to us and appeared not to know what we were saying, but later we could hear him chortle, talking to himself and laughing. "Son-of-a-bitch—son-of-a-bitch—son-of-a-bitch—hahahaha." He picked up other words, too, that were strictly American, those—shall we say—typical Army expletives of the four-letter variety. He claimed he couldn't speak English, but we began to wonder when he could isolate just a few words here and there. I talked with him, because I was rather fluent in German at that time, but he never gave me any indication that he did understand the English language.

It was here in Butgenbach that we first heard and saw Germany's "secret weapon," the "Vow Eins"—the V-1 rocket bomb. Every now and then one would quit, and we'd hear it crash and explode. We suspected Joe and his father of directing these "buzz bombs" as they were known. Then landed close to nearby targets, and someone, so it seemed, knew where those targets were.

My other recollection of Butgenbach was that is was mercilessly muddy. Tales came back from the guns that there was mud everywhere, and maneuvering was very difficult.

We stayed in Butgenbach until December 8. Then, we moved into a big schoolhouse in Mutzenich, Germany. This was a four-story building—well, three stories and a basement, which we occupied. We could look out from the building and see the enemy watching us. Opposite us was the Maginot Line—German bunkers similar to the Siegfried line we saw back in France.

One day, early in the morning, we were planning to attack the enemy, but they beat us to the punch. This was to be one of the worst days of the war for me. All of a sudden we began to hear this most horrendous whirring ROAR! They came roo roo ROO ROO ROO ROO KRANG!! KRANG!! KRANG !! KRANG!! Screaming Mimi's! It was terrifying! Enemy shells began exploding all around us! The Germans called these "nebelwerfers" (smoke throwers). We called them Screaming Mimi's because of the demoralizing, horrendous noise they made! How they ever managed to miss the building, I'll never know. Or maybe they did hit the top of the schoolhouse—we were in the basement.

The order came down to prepare to retreat. We had to pack up all of our supplies and belongings, load up the truck, and get out of there without getting hit. This was no easy task, as Pete Peterson, a healthy strapping lad from Woonsocket, South Dakota, climbed up into the truck during the intense shelling to pack the bags and battalion paraphernalia. I was in back of him, on the truck, while other members of the group handed me the items to load. In the meantime, I'll repeat, enemy shells—Screaming Mimi's—were still exploding all around us. Stress? You talk about stress—I began to see my life pass before my very eyes, not knowing whether I'd ever make it back home. Word came that the kitchen crew had already evacuated, and they were on their way to Eupen, not terribly far away. The only trouble was, they left their equipment behind! Our service battery came back and retrieved it later.

It wasn't really very long until we, too, got under way. We retreated to Eupen where we regrouped and found that most of us made it back there okay. We learned, however, that an exploding shell had killed one of our really good telephone linemen. However, our harrowing experience was over. I still can't believe that we were spared from those Screaming Mimi's, but we could still hear them coming in until we got well along down the road.

We set up our Fire Direction Center in Eupen and began directing fire almost immediately. We sent a "wall of steel"[1] back to those gerries. What good did it do? This was December 17th, the day the Germans broke through to start the Battle of the Bulge. Due to our participation in the tremendous shelling we and other artillery units stopped the onslaught through the region where we were.

On the 20th of December, we moved to Elseborn. This was just north of the path of the "Battle of the Bulge," yet just a mile or two west of what had been the front line. We were at the "Elsenborn Corner."

We stayed here a long time. We celebrated Christmas here; in fact we were strafed by one of our own planes on Christmas day! But we had many interesting experiences at Elsenborn. It grew quite cold in Elsenborn, and it snowed vigorously. We had no buildings to live in, so we dug foxholes, and that's where we lived! I had a friend with whom I shared a foxhole. We used our two shelter

---

[1] A description given us by a captured German general

halves to cover the foxhole. One night, we lit a fire at one end of the foxhole to keep us warm. As I recall, we did, indeed, keep warm, and the next day we had to get up and go to work. But apparently the smoke had backed up into our foxhole, and we both were nearly overcome by smoke inhalation. The actual result was that we both had tremendous headaches. I remember my friend complained of his headache, and they let him go back to bed. On the other hand, they couldn't dismiss both of us, so I had to stay on and compute. That was one of the worst headaches I have ever had. WOW.

Our firing patterns while we were in Elsenborn were different from the run of the mill fire missions. We did what was called "interdiction" firing. We aimed our guns at a particular crossroad which the Germans were known to use and fired our guns in a random fashion. The Germans never knew when a round (a shot, that is) would fall on or near that crossroad. Our guns were extremely accurate. Remember, they were 155 millimeter-long toms, and they had incredible accuracy up to 20 miles. Picture it this way: where would 20 miles from your home be? It's like the distance from downtown Chicago to downtown Evanston, Illinois! Now how do we know how close these rounds came? We had air observers, men who piloted piper cubs to observe our shots from the air. What fantastic observation posts! So, anyhow we knew we were hitting the targets. The enemy just never knew when they'd hit.

We worked a great part of the time while there supporting the artillery of the 1st Infantry Division. As a result, our battalion won high commendation from the artillery commander of the 1st Infantry Division, the commanding general of the 1st Infantry Division and from Major General C. R. Heubner, commander of the V Corps (Fifth Corps—also referred to as "Victor"). The men of our battalion, part of the 190th Field Artillery Group, were officially fifth Corps troops.

In January each individual went back to a rest center set up in Verviers, Belgium, for a couple of days of rest and rehabilitation (R&R). It was nice to have a nice bed, a shower, and some leisure time to shop and walk about the town for a couple of days.

Shortly after I returned from Verviers, we began moving forward again. We moved back to Mutzenich, Germany, and later on to a town called Waldorf. Lady Luck was really good to me here. I won a 10-day pass to Paris. One of our headquarters battery drivers drove me back into France to a city where I was able to board a train for the City of Light. While I was riding the train, I heard that our parachute troops had staged a landing in the Netherlands.

When I arrived in Paris, I stayed in a room on the second floor of a walk-up hotel somewhere near the Gare de Lyon, which is where I had come in. One time during the night, I heard someone trying to enter my room. Because I had locked the door, they were unsuccessful. However, I moved to another hotel to finish out my stay.

I visited the American Red Cross in Paris where I either rented, but more than likely was loaned, a bicycle to tour the city. I probably saw more of the city than anyone would on an escorted tour! My recollection of the city is that it was relatively clean. I also did many of the things that I had done the first time I was in Paris. I did, however, tour the Louvre this time, seeing with my own eyes Winged Victory and the Mona Lisa. The Louvre is a gigantic art museum, and if I ever get back to Paris, it'll be a must-see item.

My time having elapsed, I boarded the train for wherever it was I had started the journey. My driver was there to meet me, and we drove back to the battery in the town of Nichenich, Germany, where we were billeted in a house there. What I remember so distinctly about this house was the cellar full of potatoes and kohlrabi. Here it was, late March, still a lot of time until summer, and these people still had an almost full basement of two staple vegetables. Frugal folks, I'd say.

# Part IV

*Gerrys on the Run*

A FEW DAYS LATER — MARCH 25TH TO BE EXACT — it was time to move on. We left at night for some reason. Probably troop movements were coordinated from many phases of the Army. Anyway, at midnight, we crossed the Rhine River on a pontoon bridge in the shadow of the famous captured Remagen Bridge. The history book tells me it was in the town of Honningen. We traveled until about 1:30, where we dismounted in the town of Neuweid. The whole battalion rested here until April 3rd. This was like a time of renewal. Many of us got to know each other well. We did have one rather funny incident here. Well, it's funny looking back at it.

We stayed in a rather good-sized home, where,

again, the inhabitants did not stay. They would return from time to time to take care of household tasks and to do some gardening. We noticed there were a lot of chickens in the yard, and one night we decided to have one or two for dinner. I had worked on a poultry farm during a couple of summers while I was in high school, so I knew how to prepare the birds for cooking. Yeah, we had a scrumptious, delicious feast that night.

A couple of days later, a lady appeared at the door saying something about some chickens. Well, I was the fellow who spoke German, so guess whom they called to talk to this lady? It seems she was missing a couple of her chickens, and she wondered what had happened to them. Hoo boy! If anyone knew what happened to those chickens, I was the one! I remember turning around to have a quick conference with some of the other men standing around, and we decided that we didn't know where her chickens were. (Hey, c'mon now, we really didn't know where they were. We just knew where they had gone!) Did she check with people down the road? Make no mistake about it; she knew what happened to those chickens! Lucky for us, nothing came of the incident, but we didn't take any more chickens.

On April 3rd, we moved on. Our next stop was a town called Neustadt. We only stayed there over night and pushed on the next day to a town called Hohenwepel, where we stayed ready to set up in case we had to. Now, to give you an idea of how fast we were moving, Neuweid, two days before, was 187 miles back! In other words, we really had the Germans on the run!

At Hohenwepel a couple of things happened that

were either interesting or funny. The German people had been told to take their cameras and their guns. All of them—and any other types of weapons, which included swords, to the office of the Burgermeister, the Mayor. For the most part they had done that, and I tell you, there were some fancy swords turned in, swords with inscriptions of service to the military during historic battles. What happened to those weapons? We-l-l-l, they were turned over to some army agency—some of them, anyway—and I must admit, some of them somehow made their way to the United States.

While we were there, we occupied the office of the mayor—the Burgermeister. One day a man came to our office dressed in civilian clothes wanting help of some sort. He claimed he was deaf and hungry. One of our captains was a pretty astute fellow, and he went behind the man and dropped a pair of pliers onto the floor. Inasmuch as the man didn't even flinch, it was proven he was deaf. The next thing he was made to do was to take off his shoes. Aha! In the sole of his shoe, he had his "solbuch," his soldier book, the book all German soldiers carried. They needed it to be paid. So although the man was apparently deaf, he was nevertheless a soldier, so we turned him over to the military police.

Later a man came in who had formerly been the Burgermeister. He had been replaced by the German military appointee. "Why did you lose your job?" we asked. "Why didn't they appoint you to the position?"

The man and I carried on a conversation lasting at least five or six minutes, maybe even longer than that, during which time he explained how he had done some things that the German army didn't like. Occasionally I would interject an "Ah," "Ach so," "Ah, ich vehrstehe," or "doch?"

"Well, C'mon," urged our major impatiently. "What happened?"

I turned to the major and in four words gave his whole story: "Sir, he fucked up." With considerable laughter, everyone was satisfied, we found the Burgermeister to be quite friendly. There was no reason to detain him.

We left Hohenwepel on April 10, and, with a couple of stops in between, we traveled 106 miles to the city of Laucha. We had some casualties on the way to Laucha, according to my history source. Two of our trucks were ambushed by enemy guerillas. I really wasn't aware of that.

Well, on April 18, we were ordered to the city of Leipzig, where we arrived at about 8 o'clock at night. Our mission was to police the city. When we arrived, we could hear fighting still going on toward the center of the town. Many of our men guarded banks and public buildings and took prisoners, as well as weapons, and turned them over to V Corps headquarters. I don't remember exactly what I did, but I was an official translator, "ein dolmetcher" in German terms.

We moved on from Leipzig at the end of April and proceeded to the area of Bernek, stayed one day, and moved to Selb, where our guns were set up. Three days later we moved into Czechoslovakia to a town called Rommersreuth. Two days later we were told that all

German resistance would cease at midnight on May 9th. At that time, we moved to Katzengrun, and there was no further action.

The History of the 200th Field Artillery Battalion summarizes our action: "Thus, after 10 months and 29 days of fighting, the European war has ended for the 200th FIELD ARTILLERY BATTALION. During the course of our combat career, we expended 60,160 rounds of 155mm ammunition against the enemy. We participated in the initial assault on the coast of Normandy, we fired in the battle of St. Lo, we helped close and wipe out the Argentan-Falaise pocket, we helped liberate Paris, and were among the first to enter Germany. We held like a stone wall near Monschau helping to stop the German break through, then fought across Germany to take over the City of Leipzig after helping to seal the Ruhr pocket."

## Part V
*The War Ends*

THE WAR WAS OVER. OH YEAH? NOT QUITE! We still had the Japanese to contend with. My resource book ends here, so I must go it alone with my memories. Our battery moved into Czechoslovakia to the town of Sedlice (pronounced sed leet' za). I met a family in this small town, acquainted with the city of Chicago, Illinois! What are nice people like this doing in the big city of Chicago? They were friends of Chicago's mayor: "Mayor Chairmach." Chairmach? Who was he? That's the way they'd pronounce Cermak. Everyone knew Mayor

Cermak! After all, what would 22nd street in Chicago be without Mayor Cermak?

About that time I was selected to go to Pilsen, Czechoslovakia, to help draw battle maps for the Fifth Corps history across Europe. It was like drafting work, making precise figures on paper to denote various places, etc. I was qualified to do this, because I had had mechanical drawing in high school, and engineering drawing during that first year of college. I drew little boxes with the lines on them that looked like flags at particular sites. The little boxes either told what happened at a particular place, or told when something happened there. I was there at least one month, and maybe two. Anyway, when I returned to where Headquarters Battery was camped, it had to be close to September.

We thought we'd get ready to go home, but wait! The war was not over. As I mentioned earlier, we still had Japan to deal with, so we were directed to go on maneuvers and practice for deployment to the pacific theater of operation. We went on maneuvers in the Czechoslovakian "outback." Czechoslovakia is a beautiful country, both hilly and flat, with forests and farmland.

These maneuvers turned out to be another exercise in recreation. I remember this very vividly because it was just after we left our campsite that the atom bomb was dropped on Hiroshima. We couldn't believe what they were telling us! The airplane dropped this bomb in a parachute! Are you kidding? And it leveled a whole city! For real? Someone had gotten a newspaper where it was described. It was, indeed, for real. Boy, I'll tell you it made us glad we were Americans!

A couple of days later, we were again riding in our truck. We were out in the open, instead of having the "covered wagon" top over us. Someone must have had a radio because all of a sudden word came that the Japanese armistice had been signed. Whooeee!! There is joy in "Mudville" today! We returned to our bivouac location in populated Czechoslovakia. Now, for real, the war was over! And it was time to move on again.

## Part VI
*Homeward Bound*

WE MOVED INTO THE LITTLE TOWN OF POCINOVICE (pronounced Po see no veet'sa). This was a quaint little town with a very pretty church with a byzantine dome on top. Not far away, actually within walking distance—it was really a pretty long walk—was fairly good-sized town whose name I cannot remember; but all sorts of activities took place over there. There were dances, people with whom to visit, and picturesque walkways. One in particular led up a beautiful hill, on top of which were grassy areas, and trees that formed small glens that resembled very small forest preserves. We spent quite awhile in Pocinovice.

Then, in early November, my name was summoned to load up in a truck. Yea Baby! It was time to head home! My destination? Lucky Strike—Camp Lucky Strike, that is. There were camps named for cigarettes all through France. They were designed to house soldiers who were homeward bound. We stayed there until it was time to board a ship for the voyage across the ocean. It was late November that I was still in Camp Lucky Strike, because

I had Thanksgiving dinner there. The Army can conjure up an incredibly delicious feast when it wants to, I can tell you that.

Then on another day, my name was called to load up on another truck. This was to be a magnificent drive in more ways than one. The cigarette camp was on a high flat sandy mesa with not a lot of vegetation around it. It was warm and dry—actually, my kind of weather! But as the truck drove on, we came to a bluff high above the port of Marseilles. What a beautiful sight! Not only did the city lie before us, but the deep blue Mediterranean to our left was gorgeous! Hey, and there's a boat in the harbor. D'you s'pose that's waiting for me? Gosh, it's not a very big one, and the closer we drive, the smaller it gets! It was a Liberty ship—one that was hastily built to aid the shipping capacity for our country during the war. Its name was SS Exchange. Finally the truck came to a halt, and we all jumped onto the ground.

What difference did it make if it wasn't the Queen Mary? It was going to take us home! After we dismounted from the truck, we stood in a line waiting to board the ship. Hooray! Spirits were high. We were really going home! After what seemed an eternity, it was probably only a few minutes, the line began to move, and we walked up the gangplank onto the ship. It was getting toward evening, and well nigh dinnertime. Troops were the last to be loaded, and we left Marseilles about 8 o'clock. I remember watching the lights of the city disappear into the distance and into the night.

The next day was Thanksgiving—oh you thought I had Thanksgiving last week! I see. Well, you're right.

You see, the Army celebrated the day one Thursday, and the Navy celebrated it the following Thursday. So the second Thanksgiving Day was as good as the first, except we were now at sea. The Mediterranean is a most beautiful body of water. There is a deep purple hue to it, and it was so calm and peaceful.

On the third day, we passed through the Straights of Gibralter. It was a nice day with good weather, so we got a wonderful view of the rock. What an imposing sight! But as they often said in the radio program, "Kaltenmeyer's Kindergarten:" "After the moosic always comes schoosic." And after the beautiful serenity of the indigo waters of the Mediterranean, and the majestic stature of the stately Rock of Gibralter, came the lighter blue Atlantic with very rough seas!

The next day, I was assigned to K.P. (Kitchen Police)—dining room duty! I'll tell you, aboard that ship, there was a whole lot of rockin' goin' on. Sea sickness abounded! Whooeee, it was bad. I worked well in the morning, but as afternoon approached, even I was beginning to feel woozy. Well, I went to my bunk and lay down until I began to feel better. Finally, over the public address system, I heard, "T-5 Hannas, Report to the kitchen. T-5 Hannas, report to the kitchen." I went there and finished my K.P. duty without any further problems.

On another day, there was excitement on the starboard side as another ship pulled up alongside of us. Holy Cow, what was happening now? A small boat was lowered from the other ship, and three or four people came from that ship to ours. The other ship wasn't as well equipped as our SS Exchange, so they transferred a soldier with appendicitis from that ship to ours.

The rest for the voyage was uneventful, except, as I recall, we encountered rough seas most of the way: up one wave and down the next. At times I wondered if that would delay our arrival in the United States. We arrived at Hampton Rhodes, Newport News, Virginia, early one evening. I don't remember the exact date, but I know it was early December and it was COLD when we actually left the ship.

We transferred in a most orderly fashion to trucks that took us to the welcoming camp. We weren't there long, because I remember toting my duffle bag over my shoulder along a fairly long platform early the next evening to board the troop train for Camp Grant, Illinois. No Pullmans on this train; it was all coach. I remember passing through Richmond, but that's probably when I fell asleep. The next day, we were approaching northern Indiana, and if it was cold back in Newport News, it was frigid, now! Ice was on the windows, and we couldn't even see out. That was the last night aboard the train before we reached Chicago early the next morning.

In Chicago, we were detained in the Milwaukee Road coach yard. We were there quite awhile, so I called my old high school pal, Dick Williams of Evanston, who came to the train to visit. We finally left Chicago in the afternoon, and arrived at Camp Grant in time for a late dinner. I was amazed that Warren Goodlad wasn't there to greet me!

I was in Camp Grant for three days, while I had a

physical examination and some work done on my teeth. And finally I was mustered out, ...a free man ... no more soldier. Hard to believe. Now, the last day was a real tickler for my fascination with trains. The train to Chicago was a Burlington train. The railroad used suburban equipment for the run. Just think! I'd be going through my home town of Western Springs! The train was due to leave at 1:15 PM, and was to arrive in Union Station, Chicago at 4:30 PM. Well, we sat, and we sat, and we sat on that train for an hour and a half before it left. Now, get this: it left Camp Grant an hour and a half late, but it arrived in Chicago on time! That was one of the fastest train rides I have ever had. My father and my brother, Allan, were at the station to greet me. How great it was to be back with my own family again!

# EIGHT

## Dear Ajax

AFTER WORLD WAR II ENDED — Germany surrendered May 7, 1945, and Japan surrendered August 15th — it was at last time to return home. You have the background for the trip in the last section of "WWII, a Retrospective," and here's the meaning of our title: "Dear Ajax." During my time on the SS Exchange, which you may remember from the previous chapter was the ship that took me back to America, I kept a diary aboard ship across the Atlantic Ocean. Here is that diary:

*28 November 1945*
Dear Ajax,

I really don't know you, Ajax, I've never even heard of you, but Ajax sounds better than diary; so if it's okay with you, I'll use your name.

This is a rather happy day. I say rather because there were some moments when I was just plain disgusted! We were supposed to have loaded onto the trucks at eleven o'clock this morning, but the trucks didn't come until twelve thirty. I was all packed, of course, ready for one inspection after the other—that's what we were told to expect, but while traveling along on the big semi-trailer truck toward Marseilles, the strap on my musette bag broke. I tried to think of how to carry my belongings, balancing the duffel bag over one arm and balancing the bag with a broken strap with the other. This was rugged, but I managed it all successfully.

Well, we finally climbed aboard the S.S. Exchange at about 3:45 PM. We had coffee and doughnuts through the courtesy of the American Red Cross first, and as we walked up the gang plank, we were handed bags by the Red Cross worker. Boarding the ship was long and tedious, but probably only half as long as it seemed. Incidentally, the A.R.C. bags contained candy, cigarettes, playing cards, shoe polish, razor blades, and a razor.

We shoved away from the pier at 5:45 PM—just as I was stepping through the water-tight doors to descend the ladder to the mess hall for supper.

Supper was pretty good, too—that's more than I expected it to be. We had Vienna sausage and sour kraut, string beans, coffee, bread, and butter. We ate off trays and drank from porcelain cups, so my mess kit is now a thing of the past.

After supper, I went to the stern of the ship to watch Marseilles disappear into the night. We are on the way home!

*29 November 1945*
Day 1 at sea
Dear Ajax,

Was I surprised this morning! I sweated out the line for breakfast, and to my amazement there was a half grapefruit awaiting me! Besides that, we had fresh scrambled eggs, cream of wheat, coffee, bread, and butter.

Lunch was what we have been told will be regular: sandwich, cookies, and an apple. It didn't fill many of us, but dinner was good. Most of the men got turkey, but they were all out of it when we got there, so we had roast beef instead. We had mashed potatoes, peas, cranberry jelly, coffee, and bread and butter with it. The meals were good today.

We saw land almost all day today off the port (left) side. Most of the fellows seem to think it is Africa, but I don't see how it could be since we would have to travel quite far south for that. I presume it is a large group of islands out there.

The sun was shining most of the day, and made the sea look beautiful. The Mediterranean seems to be royal blue, and believe me — it looks deep!

They had a movie tonight behind #6 hatch. The Falcon in Hollywood was playing. I had seen it before, but I enjoyed it anyway.

I'm turning in early tonight because the clerk just told me I go on K. P. tomorrow afternoon at 1:00, and I will undoubtedly work until 11:00 PM! Oh, unhappy day!

*30 November 1945*
Day 2
Dear Ajax,

Here I am out under a bell clear sky with millions of stars shining brightly overhead. The ship is rocking like a rocking chair: backwards and forwards, but not from side to side. I feel like a hardened seaman tonight and have a heart full of congratulations and thanks for my stomach, which I thought was going to turn, but changed its mind and stayed peaceful.

When I got up this morning we were in the deep blue Mediterranean. Now and then through the haze we could see the outline of land, but not even my field glasses would help bring the land close enough to see. It was probably the coast of Spain we saw.

The weather was cloudy with intermittent showers, and the visibility, poor. But In spite of it all, we were able to see many sights. The weather was good to us, though, when it cleared for the highlight of the journey. Visibility became good when we came close enough to distinguish life and activity on the Rock of Gibralter. The rock is a grand sight to see. When we first saw it through the haze, we could see the northeast corner sticking straight up out of the water. Soon we could make out the cloud-like top of the rock. And as we traveled on, we could see the southern tip of it. It seemed to fall and gradually disappear into the sea. It looked something like this:

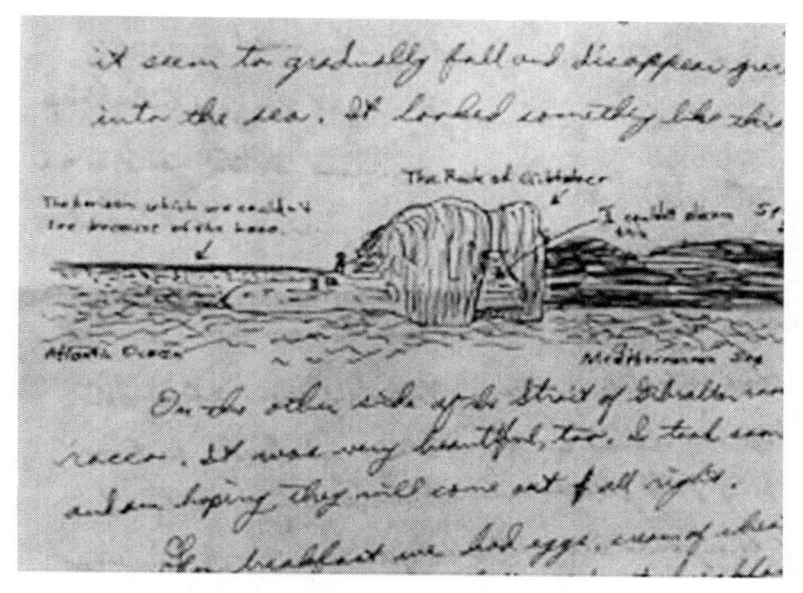

On the other side of the strait was Morocco. It was very beautiful, too. I took some pictures, and I'm hoping they will come out all right.

For breakfast, we had eggs, cream of wheat, fried potatoes, coffee, bread, and butter. We ate breakfast on the peaceful Mediterranean, but that was the last peaceful meal we ate. We ate lunch on the Atlantic, and, believe me, that Atlantic had a bit of mischief in it. We had liverwurst sandwiches, cookies, and a cup of ice cream. It all went down orderly, but many fellows didn't seem to keep themselves as well self-contained as others.

I had the misfortune of being assigned on a K.P. (Kitchen Police) detail, and I worked for about an hour cleaning out the mess hall from lunch. I was beginning to feel woozy. When I stepped up, the ship went down, and when I stepped down, the ship came up. I decided I'd better run to a porthole for air. As I took a deep breath, I distinguished in the air a strongly concentrated odor of butyric acid. I don't believe I need to tell you what was on the sill of that porthole; but I tell you—I made a rather hurried exit from the mess hall to the deck. The fresh air on deck cured me, and my stomach decided to settle again and be nice to me. Many thanks, stomach. Many thanks, indeed.

I remained outside for two hours until they sent out a call for all K.P.s to return. I served coffee for the evening meal which, incidentally, was roast beef, mashed potatoes, carrots, coffee, bread, butter, and a salad which I think was beets and onions. I only ate a roast beef sandwich, though, but I felt very well. A friend and I cleaned the coffee pot and snuck out of the mess hall for the day.

So here I am now imagining myself on the roller coaster at Riverview Park in Chicago—actually riding the waves on the S. S. Exchange!

Up until noon we had traveled 716 miles from Marseilles, 438 miles since noon yesterday.

I'm going to the movie called Harrington's Kids now, so until tomorrow, Ajax, adieu.

*1 December 1945*
Day 3
Dear Ajax,

Today is our third full day at sea. Our paper, "The Sea Breeze," said that we had traveled 1100 miles from Marseilles and 384 miles since yesterday at noon.

The sea is quite calm today—about the same as yesterday afternoon. It is a darker blue than the Mediterranean—the green seems to have disappeared. The sun was shining part of the time this morning, but went under to stay at about three this afternoon.

At about 4:30 it began to rain. Gee, I hope the water remains calm.

For breakfast this morning we had eggs, oatmeal, baked potatoes, coffee, bread, and butter. The eggs didn't look so good, so I didn't take any. I was sorry I didn't because the fellows who sat next to me said they were delicious. The rest of the breakfast was delicious, too. For lunch we had cheese sandwiches and three whole vanilla wafers. Dinner was quite a meal. We had spare ribs, dehydrated potatoes, carrots, baked beans, tomato and lettuce salad, coffee, bread, and butter. My tray was piled high, and I ate everything but the gristle of the spare ribs, the bones of which had already been removed. I think we are going to have chicken tomorrow, because we saw chicken heads and entrails being thrown over board and floating in the sea this afternoon.

The Special Service Department tonight broadcast the Army-Navy game. It came on at 6:00, and in the course of events, Army won 32 to 13.

Bed looks pretty inviting tonight. I have done nothing, but I feel as if I have had a busy day.

PS—It's strange. We don't pass through any small towns—we always used to when we moved.

*2 December 1945*
Day 4
Dear Ajax,

Here I sit on my bunk munching a chocolate bar trying to remember what happened today.

From noon yesterday until noon today, our ship traveled 387 miles making our distance from Marseilles total up to

1487 miles. I talked with one of the crew tonight—I think he is one of the officers, although I couldn't tell very well because we were at the movie, and it was dark. He told me he thought we ought to dock on the 8th. That's only six days away—not bad if we can do it.

The sea was quite choppy today, and, of course, many of the men were seasick all over again. I, personally, never felt better in my life. All day long I was in the fresh air; and when I wasn't riding at the stern, I rode the bow, and when I wasn't riding either place, I was eating—and I did plenty of that, too! I like very much to ride either end of the ship because of the up and down motion - it's like riding the roller coaster, except I save my dimes and ride free all day long.

Getting around to eating, which I mentioned above, we had hard-boiled eggs, hash, oatmeal, coffee, bread, and butter for breakfast. Lunch was the usual sandwich—cheese sandwich, today—ice cream, and a package of cookies. Dinner was a fine meal; we had fried chicken, dehydrated potatoes, peas, string beans, lettuce salad, coffee, bread, and butter, and preserved cherries. And, of course, all day long I ate beaucoup candy, peanuts, oranges, and just about anything offered to me.

Tonight, as I was eating dinner, a call came over the public address system asking for a volunteer to give some blood at the dispensary. Also, the transport surgeon was called to the radio room. It looks like we might be getting a very sick man aboard this vessel from another ship. Even though it sounds logical, it's still only rumor, but it could still be wrong. The medical department aboard ship is very good—the first night we were aboard, the transport surgeon, a Lt. Colonel, performed an appendectomy. The patient is coming along fine, too.

Tonight we had another movie. Humphrey Bogart starred in Big Shot. It was good—kinda reminded me of Saturday afternoon at the local theater back home.

Well, it's time to call it a day. Adieu!

*3 December 1945*
Day 5
Dear Ajax,

I got up early this morning and went up on deck to see if we were actually traveling with another liberty ship from which we were to take a very sick passenger. Sure enough, just ahead of us was the Samuel Asch Liberty tossing aimlessly about in the deep blue. She was signaling to our ship when I first saw her, but I steadily watched the action going on aboard our vessel, the S.S. Exchange. Soon, the ship's mate, the transport surgeon, and four other men were lowered from the boat deck in a gasoline motor powered dinghy. It was about 0630 when the party set out for the Samuel Asch.

The small craft seemed to labor as it went over first one wave then the other, and it finally reached the starboard (right) side of the liberty ship and tied up amidship. I watched the litter being lowered, slowly at first and gradually gaining speed as it went downward. The foot end of the litter dropped lower than the head, and the crew in the dinghy caught it. Presently the party with its new member left the Samuel Asch and turned toward the good ship Exchange.

When the party reached our ship, I was unable to see the litter raised aboard, but I did see the party lifted to the boat deck.

Through my glasses, I watched the Samuel Asch list toward her port side, and lift her nose into the air. She gave three short toots on her whistle and headed forward toward the horizon.

It was fifteen to twenty minutes before we steamed onward, but when we began, it wasn't long until we reached full speed. Two hours later, the Samuel Asch was on the horizon behind us.

The man who was brought aboard was Ira Jennings who is stricken with a hemorrhaging peptic ulcer; as fate would have it, the patient was with the 200th Field Artillery Battalion aboard the liberty ship. He will be in the United States days ahead of the 200th battalion, which was my outfit originally!

Counting the retarded speed during the operation of transfer, which actually began last night at midnight, we covered 353 miles from noon yesterday to noon today. Now we are 1840 miles from Marseilles, and we are still headed for Hampton Roads, Virginia.

The sea was considerably calmer today, and that made all the meals more popular. Therefore each man didn't get quite as much to eat. For breakfast, we had scrambled fresh eggs, bacon, wheatena, boiled fresh potatoes, coffee, bread, and butter. Lunch brought luncheon meat sandwiches, pickles, cookies, and an apple. Dinner wasn't as good as usual, but still was quite good: spare ribs, dehydrated potatoes, baked beans cabbage, lettuce, orange, coffee, bread, and butter.

After dinner we had another movie. I was tired, so I went up onto the forward gun deck over the bow and slept for about an hour beneath the stars. It is a really pleasant journey when we aren't doing some kind of dirty detail.

*4 December 1945*
Day 6
Dear Ajax,

The mighty Atlantic loosed its fury upon us today as we experienced the roughest waters of our voyage to date. I awoke just in time to make the chow line for breakfast and could only stumble as if drunk to the mess hall. After a breakfast of hash, hard-boiled eggs, cream of wheat cereal, coffee, bread, and butter, I went up on deck to ride the storm. The waves were like mountains of water, although some of the biggest might have been a mere thirty feet high. As the stern reared high into the air, it gave us the thrill of our lives, and then we sank until the water came up almost to the deck. The high waves in the wake hid the horizon, and then, again, into the air we soared. The propeller came out of the water and threw a salt spray far behind and to the side and roared as we gracefully slipped low again. This continued all through the day, but we couldn't ride in the open much in the afternoon because the powerful wind carried rain with it.

Many say the rough weather started early this morning, but in spite of it, we traveled 384 miles between noon yesterday and noon today. We have traveled 2,224 miles from Marseilles and are still scheduled to dock at Hampton Roads, Virginia (subject to change).

For lunch we had luncheon meat sandwiches, an orange. and a cup of ice cream. For dinner, we had stew, spinach, white-waxed beans, celery, bread, butter, and coffee. I made away with beaucoup celery and ate on deck after I finished the rest of my dinner in the mess hall.

The movie scheduled for tonight was canceled because of bad weather, so it's early to bed tonight.

*5 December 1945*
Day 7
Dear Ajax,

The sea has again become quiet and the speed of the ship has increased. We only traveled 345 miles noon to noon, which means we have left 2569 miles behind us on our voyage.

Almost all day dragged, and as we come closer and closer to port I begin to think more and more about home in anticipation of what I will do when I get home. It's hard to realize that I will be able to turn the dial of a radio and choose a program to please me, to drive a family automobile—not the CO's jeep—and to dress the way I see fit seems almost out of this world. I think all the dreaming boils down to the fact that I am growing weary of watching the sea.

I just barely got to the mess hall in time for breakfast this morning. We had fresh scrambled eggs, oatmeal, hash, coffee, bread, and butter. I was on time for lunch, though, with its sandwiches and apple. Dinner was served seemingly early, and we had good old corned beef and cabbage, dehydrated potatoes, lettuce, coffee, bread, and butter.

After supper, the movie Dragon Seed was shown in the amphitheater by hatch #6. It was a very philosophical piece of propaganda. I laughed to myself in the spot where food was thrown upon the ground by the Japanese soldiers. The soldiers laughed when the hungry Chinese people scrambled for the food. This particular scene was to make us hateful toward the enemy soldiers, but how could I hate them for that when I would watch the American soldiers do the same with cigarettes in war-torn, cigarette-craving Europe with laughter? The hungry look upon the faces of the women wanting Japanese reminded me of the American "combat sojer" who believes the world owes him so much. I cannot hate. I just look upon them as undesirables and prefer to have no dealings with any of them.

I just remembered a pair of words the French people always say before going to bed: "Bon soir."

*6 December 1945*
Day 8
Dear Ajax,

We woke up early this morning and watched the sun rise. It was a very beautiful dawn with all colors on the red side of the rainbow flashing upon the azure sky and being reflected upon the ultramarine water of the mighty Atlantic. It was foretelling of the weather to follow throughout the day. At about ten o'clock the sky became cloudy and a drizzle began to fall, and most of the day was spent behind the misty walls in a clouded sanctum all our own. In fact, the bad weather even canceled the showing of the daily film this evening.

We were expecting to eat first this morning, but much to our chagrin, we didn't eat until last as the cooks and K.P.s had overslept. Thereby we had a long wait for breakfast. The meal consisted of ground beef, hard-boiled eggs, wheatena, boiled potatoes, coffee, bread, and butter. Since the meal was late, the noon meal was omitted due to the necessity of preparation of the evening meal. Supper consisted of pork chops, mashed dehydrated potatoes, bean soup, purple cabbage, coffee, bread, and butter.

This monotonous day came to a close very early tonight. We are well on toward the close of our journey, though, having traveled 356 knots during the current period making the total distance traveled 2925 knots. I happened to be talking to one of the special service men aboard ship who told me the man from the navigation room had calculated that we should dock between 0001 and 1200 Sunday, 9 December at Hampton Roads, Virginia.

*7 December 1945*
Day 9
Dear Ajax,

We ate a fine breakfast this morning: scrambled fresh eggs, bacon, fried potatoes, cream of wheat cereal, an orange, coffee, bread, and butter. After breakfast I was detailed to sweep the deck from bow to stern.

Fifteen of us, two with shovels and the rest with brooms, completed the task in less than a half hour. We had a rough sea and a strong wind to work against while we were on the bow, but the rest of the ship was quiet, although it rocked and rolled along.

The waves of the ocean were not as high as they were a couple of days ago, but they swept faster from the port bow to the starboard stern causing the ship to rock and roll more fiercely than before. Then came the rain—and in torrents. It battered the sea, the ship, and most of the men aboard the ship. It was the worst storm I have ever seen because the wind brought the rain at a very high velocity. When the rain stopped, the sun shone again, but the sea remained rough, and the wind continued to blow with anger.

Just after the rain stopped it was time to eat lunch, which consisted of cheese sandwiches, cookies, and ice cream. It was also time to take the readings on mileage. We covered 404 knots in the day, bringing the total knots traveled from Marseilles to 3329. I speak of this in knots because I checked the publication "Sea Breeze," which is my only source, and the figures are either erroneous, or else erroneously labeled. Since the information for the paper is received from the navigation room, I believe the figure to be erroneously labeled. 3329 knots is equal to 3835 miles.

We cleaned the decks again this afternoon and after that, at supper. We had meat loaf, mashed dehydrated potatoes, stewed tomatoes, and bread, baked beans, coffee, bread and butter.

The movie scheduled to be shown tonight was canceled because of the bad weather, so the day ended soon.

*8 December 1945*
Day 10
Dear Ajax,

After another day of stormy weather during which two men aboard were slightly injured, we have finally reached a hole in the clouds through which the millions of stars in our universe are shining. This afternoon the ship was rocking roughly, and after the stern had settled in the water after rearing over one high wave, another washed the deck causing two men to lose their balance and fall upon the steel plate deck. One man received a bump and a scratch on his nose, while the other man injured his leg. After the man with the scratched nose got up the buddies of the other man helped him to safety. Seriousness of the leg injury was not known, but the stern has been roped off as out of bounds to troops.

The stormy weather has impeded our speed greatly. The "Sea Breeze" said today that we traveled only 268 knots or miles or whatever unit the navigation office seems to want to make it. Since it was labeled miles today, I'll say miles. Therefore we have traveled 3597 miles from Marseilles, France, the distance, nautically, because of misuse of terminology cannot be considered correct. What do you suppose would be entered into the ship's log? I would like to know.

For breakfast this morning, we had hash, hard-boiled eggs, oat meal, coffee, bread, butter, and jam. We had sandwiches, ice cream, and an apple for lunch; and pork, dehydrated potatoes, spinach cabbage, coffee, bread, butter and an apple for supper.

The movie, Along Came James, has been canceled for the third time. The day is ending soon again tonight because I have been detailed for K. P. again tomorrow afternoon.

*9 December 1945*
Day 11
Dear Ajax,

Almost everyone was on deck this morning because, as if by magic, the sea had become a calm bed for our ship, and the sun was shining brightly. A warm breeze blew swiftly over the bow from the port side as we began to speed onward toward our destination, Hampton Roads, Virginia, USA!

I took two pictures of the ship before reporting for K.P. at 1300 hours. My job was to start right in to wash pots and pans, etc, in the kitchen, but not feeling like working, I made an exit and returned to my bunk where I spent most of the time of the detail.

We traveled 326 miles today, making our total 3923 from Marseilles. We are expected to arrive in port at midnight tonight and dock tomorrow morning. This battalion, the 190th FABn, will be the first off the ship at 0900 hours.

For breakfast today, we had scrambled eggs and tomatoes, wheatena, fried potatoes, coffee, bread, and butter. Sandwiches, cookies, and an orange were for lunch; stew, spaghetti, peas, coffee, bread, butter, and an apple were the constituents of our supper.

With this, I close the diary of an eventful, monotonous voyage. I thank you, Ajax, for letting me use your name.

# NINE

## The Midnight Ride of the Royal Palm

You know; I have never considered myself a sentimentalist. The fact is, I usually look reality squarely in the eye and take whatever comes. Reality is the essence of preparing for the future, which I do with great contentment, but I guess I'm human enough to be sentimental at least once in a while. Take the case that did happened a few years back when I experienced a chronic attack of nostalgia. Whoa! How that took me back—more than fifty years!

We were in the process of moving from Illinois to Tennessee. I was heading south with a trailer-load of our belongings, and I was clipping right along in northern Indiana. Now, when I'm hauling a trailer, I fantasize that I'm a railroad engineer with a train behind me. After all, I check the "train" before I leave the depot (home), and just after my departure, like a good engineer, I check to see that the brakes are working right. I set my sights into the distance and ease the throttle up to cruising speed. I also set an ETA (Expected Time of Arrival) for the ultimate destination, as well as for places in between.

In this case, our main line was Interstate 65, and at this point, we were on the outskirts of La Fayette,

Indiana. I-65 tends to wiggle its way around the east side of La Fayette, and it was while we were negotiating the hills into the valley of the mighty Wabash River that this nostalgia attack reared its rather delightful head.

You see; I spent several years in La Fayette both before and after World War II. I went to Purdue University there. Now, in those days, I traveled between Chicago and La Fayette by train—on the Big Four—the Cleveland, Cincinnati, Chicago, and St. Louis Railroad, then part of the New York Central System. The Big Four must have done the New York Central proud with its fast schedules and excellent on-time performance. It ran four trains a day between Chicago and Cincinnati, Ohio. Three of those trains were The James Whitcomb Riley, the "flagship" of the fleet; the Carolina Special; and the Royal Palm. The fourth train was a local that stopped everywhere. I don't think it had a name. Maybe they called it "The Fast Mail" or something like that.

Now, I usually rode the Carolina Special to Chicago from Purdue if I got off in the morning. It left La Fayette at about 10:30 and arrived in Chicago at 1:00, but more than likely, I left La Fayette at 2:00 PM aboard the streamlined James Whitcomb Riley and arrived in Chicago at 4:15. The Riley shaved fifteen minutes off the usual 2½ hour trip.

The James Whitcomb Riley was state of the art for those days. The cars were sleek, shiny, stainless steel, streamlined coaches, some built by the E.G.Budd Company and some by the Pullman Company. It had a full diner and a rounded-end observation car with a speedometer mounted just above the rear door, showing how fast the train was going. The Riley was always a fun train to ride. In those days—the mid to late nineteen forties—the locomotive was one of the famous Class "J" Hudsons except that the Riley's engine had a streamlined air foil done in grey and red. Silver discs covered the drive wheels. For some reason or other, you never heard much about the James Whitcomb Riley. Instead New York Central fans preferred talking about the Chicago-to-Detroit Mercury, which was not nearly as nice a train, but it had a similarly streamlined locomotive.

All the other Big Four trains were whisked along by the unsophisticated NYC workhorse, that incredible class "J" Hudson. The "J" was simply the railroad's classification. "Hudson" meant that it had four wheels under the cylinders, six driving wheels, and four wheels under the cab and firebox. It was described as "4-6-4." Many railroads had Hudson-type locomotives, The New York Central Hudsons were the most famous.

Now, if you were in Chicago when one of the Big Four trains arrived at Central Station on the lakefront, you'd think you were watching an Illinois Central train come in. You see: the Big Four westbound passenger trains went only as far as Kankakee, Illinois, with New York Central engines. Then an Illinois Central locomotive came onto the point to take the train its last 45 miles to Chicago on the Illinois Central main line. For some reason or other, the Kankakee change-over was always a bottle neck. If the train arrived in Chicago late, it was generally because of the delay in Kankakee.

Trips home to Chicago were usually on Friday: good trips with our thoughts painting delightfully romantic images of impending weekend dates with our ever-beautiful queens waiting for us. But the trips were also great fun because, in those days, the trains almost always outran the automobile traffic that ran on U. S. Highway 52 alongside the railroad.

Now let me take a minute or two to describe the geography of the beginning of the trip because when we return on our famous midnight ride, you'll be able to picture our last few minutes of that ride as we return to La Fayette. The passenger depot in La Fayette, Indiana, was built on a convex curve. We could always hear the train approaching, but we couldn't see it until it was just about into the station. At this point, the curve is on flat land.

As we climb aboard and settle into one of those roomy, comfortable seats on the coach of the Carolina Special, the engineer gives a strong shot of steam to the booster, and we feel the train ease slowly out of the station. (The booster is a tiny little steam engine underneath the firebox. When it's energized, it causes the train to very gradually and smoothly ease out of a station.) We curve left across the Wabash River through a steel truss bridge. Beyond the river, we continue to curve to the left and then to the right. As we turn to the right, we start to climb a steep grade out of the Wabash valley. When we start that climb, we can feel that "J" locomotive give a powerful tug as our engineer gives it everything. For at least five or six minutes we continue to climb out of the valley. We pass the Purdue University airport on our right, and we pick up speed as we level off a bit. Then another hill lies ahead of us, and we continue to feel the power as we climb to the summit at Montmorency. We turn slightly to the left, and as we do, we see U.S. Highway 52 on our right, the highway we will follow through Otterbein, Fowler, and on to Earl Park. We're amazed to see the speed we have reached while climbing, and now we dash to Kankakee, 75 miles away.

How fast are we traveling? Well, let me share with you some railroad lore I used to enjoy. I loved to stand in the vestibules between the cars and listen to the endless song the wheels and rails would play as we sped along. Now don't laugh. I'll bet not many modern drummers can play the rhythm those six-wheeled Pullman trucks made as they clicked across the rail joints. As our rate of speed increases, as we pass over street crossings, and as we pass over railway turn-out frogs, we have a beat with intoxicating syncopation! As we go faster, the beat goes on...but the beat changes. After the train exceeds 60 miles an hour, we no longer hear all the wheels click over the rails; instead, we're going so fast, we only hear one distinctive beat from each side of the train.

So at fast speeds, we can very easily tell how fast the train is going. You see; each rail is 39 feet long, so there are 135 clicks in a mile. Using a watch with a second hand, we count every other beat (counting, therefore, only one side of the train). If we count 135 beats in a minute's time, we know we are traveling at 60 miles an hour. If we count the 135 beats in 45 seconds, then we compute the speed to be 80 miles an hour; believe me, between Montmorency, Indiana, and Kankakee, Illinois, we did 80 miles an hour most of the way!

Now you have the basic elements for what began to go through my mind as I sped along Interstate 65 in Indiana with my own "two-car train" on my way to Tennessee. As we came to a hill descending into the valley of the Wabash River, I checked my "train" through the mirror, and saw it tracking marvelously well; I was planning to make La Fayette for lunch, and we were right on time, when all of a sudden I was struck with uncontrollable, historical take-me-back-to-the-good-old-days fantasy.

My mind went back to when I'd ride the Royal Palm back to school from Chicago in the late 1940s. At 10:00 the Royal Palm eased out of Central Station, Chicago, for La Fayette, Indianapolis, Cincinnati, and destinations in Florida. The train was scheduled through La Fayette at 12:30 AM. The Illinois Central Railroad took us to Kankakee, where we changed our steed to one of those fabled 4-6-4 "J"s. Now, as always, we left Kankakee behind schedule, which meant we had to make the time up somewhere. It seemed as if that train had to arrive in Indianapolis (a division point) right on the money, so our trip was always fast.

By the time we were a half hour out of Kankakee, almost everyone was asleep. People slouched against the windows, slid down in their seats, and some even hung over into the aisle. For some unexplained reason, I can remember the conductor who worked that train. He was a short, dour fellow with a round cherubic face and wire-rimmed glasses. He was an amazing man because in spite of a pitch black night, shades down in the coach, he knew when to get the people ready to get off at La Fayette. I could never sleep on a speeding train because there were too many things for me to think about: How fast are we going? Where are we now? How close to schedule are we? I knew that train was slicing through northern Indiana at better than 80 miles an hour. I also knew almost every inch of track and where we were as we passed through Fowler and Otterbein. I knew, too, when I felt the train lurch to the right that we were taking the curve at Montmorency, and then we were starting our wild descent into the Wabash valley where La Fayette is nestled.

With crystal clarity, I can still picture this cherubic conductor agonizing his way through the coach aisle — first squeezing past this person, then maneuvering around one or two others, grabbing for one seat handle after another sloshing along the aisle.

"La-a-a-ay Fa-a-ayette!" he called out as his glasses cling precariously to his nose. "LA-a-a-ay Fa-a-ayette This way out, please!" I can still feel the air gently set the brakes as he skillfully rouses the sleeping passengers.

The La Fayette passengers began to collect themselves while the train was still clamoring downhill at yet more than 65 miles an hour. Then came the curve to the left at the Purdue airport. Whoa! Hang on! If you were not braced you'd lose your balance. The planes and the hangers flashed by, and about then he hit the brakes hard. The whir of the brake shoes against the steel wheels was almost deafening. On that last downhill plunge, we began to wonder if our Royal Palm could slow down enough to stop!

But before we knew it, we had indeed slowed, and the steel trusses of the Wabash River bridge passed lazily by our window. The wheel clicks were then in groups of three telling us we were almost there. Click-click-click, click-click-click they resounded on the floor of the bridge. Slowly, we curved to the right, and Mr. "J" coaxed us to an amazingly smooth, graceful stop. Finally, we heard Tushshshshsh, and we glanced at our watch and saw—we were right on time! How'd he do that? We left Kankakee fifteen minutes late!

It was, indeed, 12:30 AM when we parted company. I wonder how many other hills, curves, time-binds, and track woes the Royal Palm would endure before she arrived in Florida.

I know she doesn't do it now, though, for, alas, the Cleveland, Cincinnati, Chicago, and St. Louis Railroad exists no more. In many places, the tracks aren't even there any more. All that's left are the memories of a once-proud fleet of speeding trains that raced amazingly with excellent fast schedules and unbelievably on-time accuracy. The Royal Palm, The Carolina Special, the James Whitcomb Riley—yes even the Fast Mail—were all trains that deserved to survive. We hope Amtrak will come back to that kind of performance.

Well, back to reality, and to our trip to Tennessee. Presto! I realized I had already crossed the Wabash River with my "two-car train." Had I been asleep? No—just daydreaming. But the bridge I just crossed was not that marvelous Warren truss bridge, but rather the flat, wide concrete roadway that hardly even let me know I crossed a bridge! Up ahead loomed State Route 26. I looked at my watch, and it's 12:30, by golly. I was right on time! La-a-a-ay Fa-a-ayette! Lunch never tasted so good.

# TEN

## Philharmonia?...Yessir!

MY FAVORITE ACTIVITIES IN COLLEGE were things I did on the radio station. It was "WBAA, The Voice of Purdue." If I ever continued with "West Lafayette, Indiana," I was subject to a mild but friendly dressing down from the Chief Announcer, Johnny DeCamp. Now don't misunderstand, I thought the World of Johnny DeCamp—and I still do, even though I haven't seen him in years. However, the protocol of the station identification announcement was simply, "This is WBAA, the Voice of Purdue, West Lafayette."

I had a couple of other admonishments from the chief over the three years I was involved in the station. For example, we had a series of what we, today, would call PSA's—Public Service Announcements. These "PSA's" were called "World Facts." They were short short short descriptions of facts about other countries of the world. They were fun to read, and they really were enlightening. Considering the world fact had to be given within the space of 30 to 45 seconds, they were quite well done. I don't know who wrote them, but for the most part, they were really good. However, once in a while they were somewhat dry.

So I used my "Henry Aldrich" voice—a somewhat falsetto voice mimicking a character formerly on commercial radio—on the broadcast to ask a question that led into the world fact. I would answer the question in my own voice. I thought it was quite effective. So did the engineers—the men who sat behind the studio glass window making the radio station work. Henry Aldrich was a sitcom I listened to growing up. His mother would call, "Henry? Henry Aldrich!" And always in a rather thin, somewhat high-pitched voice would come the answer, "Coming mother!"

But Johnny DeCamp didn't see it the way I did. "If we let you do that, others would try it, and it would make a mockery of the World Facts." That's creativity squelched, but, you know, I really didn't mind that, largely because Johnny was right.

Now, I actually had a specialty on WBAA. It was classical music. My two programs were the afternoon "Symphony Hour" and the evening "Dinner Hour." For each of these programs the music library lady would give me a list of selections to be played. Her list had the times it took to play each piece. It was my job to announce these selections and make certain the program timed out correctly. I have never been good at ad-libbing—that is, just talking my way through a program without a script. I tried that once and failed miserably, or should I say, I learned a very positive lesson from the very negative experience. I had also listened to other people who had done these programs, and ended the program in the middle—or at least toward the exciting end of a favorite selection. So I wrote scripts to introduce each piece. Virtually every program I planned came out exactly on time.

I spent much time in the library reading about the composers, the artists, and sometimes about the featured works themselves. Now, most of the artists were clearly identifiable. There was one group of musicians, however, that caused criticism for the WBAA classical program announcers, whoever we were. Everyone has heard of the London Philharmonic Orchestra, but every now and then we'd feature a work played by the London Philharmonia Orchestra. I don't know how many times I had to explain to my classmates that there really was a Philharmonia Orchestra. They took me at my word, because they knew I had researched all of the announcements I made.

The crowning explanation came one morning in English class. I was sort of lazing in my seat while still paying attention to my Professor of English as he was imparting some sort of sage information. He really had interesting presentations regarding the English language. Well, I don't remember what brought this incident about. Maybe he saw me slouching, which he might not have liked, but he took off on the "unprofessional presentation" of classical music announcements on our radio station, WBAA. He knew I was one of the major classical specialists. And in front of the class, without mentioning my name, he looked directly at me and openly scoffed and sneered: "London Philharmonia!...Really!... Everyone knows it's the London Philharmonic."

This was a dressing down I wasn't going to take. I am usually a very respectful person, but for some reason or other courage took over and in a very firm, matter-of-fact fashion; with complete authority in my voice, I blurted out, "There is a London Philharmonia Orchestra. The Philharmonia Orchestra is made up of members of the Philharmonic. It's tantamount to the Boston Pops, The Chicago Ravinia Festival Orchestra, or the orchestra that plays at Wolf Trap in Virginia!"

Ever see a defeated college professor?

The lesson I learned here was that if you're sure you know your facts, and you can sound off with conviction and authority, you can probably kill a dragon!

# ELEVEN

## My Entry into the Realm of Insurance

For most of my working days, I was an Independent Insurance Agent. I enjoyed my career. It was constantly a learning experience, and it was most fulfilling when I knew I was a good help to someone. How I started in the independence of it was rather fascinating—at least to me—as I look back over my life. There were a lot of incidents that literally led me to become just what I wanted to be. Here's how it all began.

I was personnel director for a delightful firm known as the H. P. Smith Paper Company in the Clearing Industrial District in Chicago. The company coated paper for various uses. They were a supplier to the meat packing industry with wax-coated papers for wrapping meat during shipment.

Well, "times they were a-changin'" as the saying goes; the need for waxed-coated paper diminished, and the need for plastic-coated papers was growing. The change over from wax to plastic required changing machinery. As you can imagine, this took a great deal of money, so, along with many others in the company, I was downsized. Holy Cow! I lost my job!

One of my responsibilities as personnel director was the safety program. I had been successful in preventing industrial accidents, which the company noted, and which the company's insurer also noted. The result of this was that the insurance company which wrote H. P. Smith's workers' compensation insurance asked me to go with them to be one of their representatives—to be a salesman, in other words.

I joined the insurance firm and enjoyed extensive product and sales training, and set out to try to sell workers' compensation insurance and general liability insurance to industrial firms in the city of Chicago. I was a complete flop. Now, because I hadn't sold much insurance for that insurance company, they felt I should be let go because of my inability to sell. I really didn't know what I was going to do.

LUCKY CAREER BREAK NUMBER 1

But one of the companies I sold coverage to was the Lorenz Garment Factory. They made ladies undergarments for Sears Roebuck and Company. One day the telephone rang, and Mrs. Lorenz called me from the garment factory. She said, "I understand you are no longer with the big insurance company."

"That's correct, Mrs. Lorenz," I replied.

And before I could say any more, she said, "Well, we don't care what company you represent now, we want you to be our insurance agent. That's why we bought our insurance from you in the first place."

You know that I couldn't let her down, so I told her, "Well, I thank you for your loyalty, and I'll get an insurance quotation for you. I'll try to get back to you next week."

Hoo Boy! Whether I liked it or not, I was still in the insurance business! I looked up the addresses of a few companies in Chicago and went in to see Mr. Dale Frye of Employers Mutual Casualty Co of Des Moines, Iowa. I told Mr. Frye my work history and pointed out I had a problem in that I needed workers' compensation and general liability coverage for the Lorenz Garment Company. Well, I went home with a set of rate manuals for Employers Mutual Casualty Company and a promise to have the garment company surveyed for coverage.

Everything worked out well, and I drove back to the Lorenz Garment Company with a firm quotation for their workers' compensation insurance. They wrote a check for the insurance, and I was in business! Not only that, I was able to solicit insurance business for other companies. Just incidentally, the relationship with Employers Mutual of Des Moines turned out to be successful, profitable, satisfying, and long-lasting!

**LUCKY BREAK NUMBER 2**

Soon after I had established my connection with Employers of Des Moines, my father and I went to the men's club meeting at the church where I had grown up. There we talked with a neighbor who asked what I was doing "these days." The neighbor, Mr. Eldon Link, had always been very friendly toward our family. Slowly, thinking in a positive frame of mind, I answered his question.

"Well," I began, "I have just gone into the insurance business as an independent agent."

"Wonderful!" he exclaimed. "I am with Motor Vehicle Casualty Company in Elmhurst. I want you come see me, and I'll set you up with an agency in our company. We write auto insurance for the average person. Our rates are really competitive. You'll like the company."

Mr. Link was the corporate secretary of this lovely company, so obtaining an agency connection was a forgone fact! Indeed, he did set me up as a company agent, and I had a company to write automobile insurance for both good driving people and for folks without a past full of accidents and traffic tickets. It's always best if you can write insurance directly with a company, because commissions are bigger, and the direct connection with the company helps in getting customers' claims settled properly. Well, like it or not, I was set up and running, and able to sell good insurance at fair, reasonable rates to my friends and to my clients. This business relationship also turned out to be satisfying, profitable, and long-lasting.

As a part time job, I worked for a producer of slide shows in Chicago, and through him, I met an agent who handled a completely full line of insurance. He was very happy to broker insurance for me. Now for me to "broker" through him meant that I would sell insurance to someone for whom it might be difficult to place in one of my direct companies. I therefore had a market for "tough" cases.

Now, I was also driving a taxi cab for extra cash to live on, and there were one or two cab customers who asked about buying insurance. One of my first clients, whom I had met while driving the taxi, was a young lady who had just bought a new car. This was an interesting case, because before I could get a policy issued, I issued her a "binder of insurance" which my brokerage friend had authorized me to do. Almost immediately this lady's sister drove my client's car and stuck a pedestrian. When my client called me to report the accident, she asked if she was covered.

This was my first experience with a binder, so I told her I was quite sure she was covered. The next day I checked with the brokerage man, and all of us were relieved to find out that all was well, and my client was, indeed, covered, and the claim was paid.

One day, a friend whom I had met at church, John Ackerman by name, telephoned me. "My homeowners insurance policy is coming up for renewal soon, and I'm wondering if you could save me some money." There was a definite lesson learned in dealing with Mr. and Mrs. Ackerman, and I'll tell you more about that in another chapter.

Most of the time, things went fairly routinely. But every now and then, the world would turn upside down! Generally, trouble came when someone couldn't understand the basis for paying claims on things like automobiles, homes, or machinery. The reason a person insured was to protect himself against loss by fire, theft, or other tragedy. Now, you have to understand that claims were paid on the basis of the actual cash value of the damaged items at the time of the loss. Actual Cash Value was determined by when the item was purchased, how much was paid for it at the time, and how old it is at the time of the tragedy. This caused more misunderstanding and disagreement than almost anything else when a claim was settled. Here's what happened with a fire loss that happened to a friend of mine.

One day, I sold a fire insurance policy to a friend I'll call Henry (not his real name). Now, understand that in selling the policy to my friend, Henry, I had to make sure he understood I was selling him an amount of coverage that approximated at least 80% of the total value of everything he was insuring. Somehow, that message escaped Henry, and he thought he was buying fire insurance like you buy life insurance. You know –like a total amount if something happened. He bought a $50,000 fire insurance policy to protect his printing business.

Wouldn't you know, a fire broke out in the building where Henry had his printing establishment! The insurance adjuster visited Henry promptly, and totaled up the value of his printing press, unused paper stock, and finished orders. To Henry, the value of his machinery and paper stock and finished orders tallied about $150,000.00 –far more than the amount for which he was insured. Fortunately, the adjuster called me, and asked how it was I had sold Henry a policy so grossly under insuring him. Believe me. For me, it was like being struck by a bolt of lightning! I knew I had sold Henry the proper coverage.

I had to contact Henry's former business partner to get an accurate value of the printing press, and I contacted other people to establish other proper values. Otherwise, instead of getting a $50,000 settlement for his claim, he'd have received 1/3 of that amount, because he had over-stated his values at an amount which made it look as though he had only 1/3 the amount of fire insurance coverage he should have had. When we worked out the proper values, it turned out he had just the right amount of coverage, and he, indeed, received the full $50,000 settlement. Now, that took leadership—believe me—and some frazzled nerves, too!

I prided myself on helping people file claims on their automobile insurance. Since it only took me a few minutes to fill out the necessary forms, I did that for them. It would take the client some time to figure out how to complete the forms. I even went to the police station and obtained the necessary police reports. I wanted to make sure the claims were filed correctly to speed up the claim settlement. One of my clients was very surprised when I showed up on the scene of his accident before the police did. In a great measure, I was "taking care of my flock." Indeed, I was their leader.

The many triumphs I experienced as an independent insurance agent were very fulfilling, and my servicing was a very important ingredient. The sad note to all of my career in insurance is that now, in the early 2000s, I wouldn't be able to enjoy the industry the way I did back in the 1900s. The reason is that today to be in the insurance industry requires a person to be a specialist. One must either be a sales person, a claims person, or someone in a specialized branch of the industry. I am so thankful to have been an independent insurance agent when I was!

# TWELVE

## Leadership Turns Up Where It's Least Expected

FOR MOST OF MY WORKING CAREER, I was an independent insurance man. I enjoyed it very much. For one thing, I was able to help people when adversity struck, and for another, I made a decent—although by no means, any kind of fabulously rich—living from it. My family and I lived comfortably.

In the last chapter, I told you how I got started in the insurance world. It was, indeed, a rewarding career. I'm not talking just about the commissions I received for the sales I made—as there were so many things I learned about people, and about myself. I described how Mrs. Lorenz had asked me to be their insurance man. I should have seen the roll of a professional agent then, but I guess there was just too much that I had to learn first, until...

Until one day, a friend whom I had met at church, John Ackerman, telephoned me: "My homeowners insurance policy is coming up for renewal soon Warren," he told me, "and I'm wondering if you could save me some money."

"I'd sure like the opportunity to try," I assured him. "When is a good time for me to come see you?" I asked.

"Well, let's say next Tuesday evening at 7:30."

So I went to see John and his wife, Betty; I had known her in school days. She was just a year or two ahead of me. I had my rate books and sample policies and everything I needed to make sure I could save money for my friends.

As one would expect, the sales interview was very friendly, and I gave them figures that looked pretty thrifty. "Well," he said. "This is much less than I am paying now, but is this the best policy for me to own? You know, Warren, we called you, because we need your expertise to help us get the best protection we can."

Then came the most important words I have ever heard in all of my career in the insurance industry: "What I'm saying is, we need your leadership in helping us to select the right coverage for our needs." That rang so loudly in my mind, It was a by-word for me for the rest of my days in the insurance business—"We need your leadership." I was forever reminded of my place as an independent insurance agent. How true! I was, indeed, the leader of the people who bought insurance from me.

Well, I ended up selling John and Betty the same type of homeowners insurance I had for myself. It was a good deal more money than the "money-saving" policy I showed him at first. Yes, I came away from that meeting with a new piece of business, and with the most important lesson I ever learned as an independent agent. The key word is leadership, and it turned up where I least expected it.

Leadership played important roles in the case of my friend, Henry, whose printing company burned, which I described in that last chapter. Believe me! That $50,000.00 settlement took leadership!

And there was the case of the college administrator who attended a bowling party one night and had just little bit too much to drink. He was arrested for "Driving Under the Influence." I don't remember what company had written his automobile insurance, but whoever it was, they cancelled him. His wife called me and told me the whole story, so I met with them and designed a program of making sure these lovely people would be adequately covered. I went over each step: for the first three years, we would have to use a company known as a "substandard" company, because they had a very bad reputation for paying claims, and yet they charged high premiums. They were this way because they would insure high-risk clients. Then we would use a standard insurer as long as we needed, and then I'd put them back into my preferred risk company, my favorite company. Well, I kept constant contact with these people, and we followed the program all the way through. I was, indeed, their leader, and they were very well pleased!

Every month I mailed an insurance newsletter that I personally wrote telling about developments in the insurance world. The paper was called "The Fireside Chat." It was another form of leadership.

I prided myself on helping people file claims on their automobile insurance. Since it took me only a few minutes to complete the necessary forms, I did it for them, because it would take the client time to figure out how to answer all those sometimes complicated questions on claim forms and on police reports. I was always mindful of my roll as leader of those who bought insurance through my agency

Unfortunately, as time wore on, commercial enterprises and community departments became aware of the need for claiming privacy. This meant I was no longer able to get access to police reports. In my opinion, "privacy" has turned out to be one of the dumbest scams ever conceived. No one has privacy if somebody really wants to find out something about us.

Anyway, as an independent insurance agent I experienced many triumphs that were very fulfilling, and leadership was a very important ingredient. Who'd have thought it?

# THIRTEEN

## Don't Call Me Sir, *%#@#&* It!

NOT LONG AFTER I GRADUATED FROM COLLEGE, and after I had worked for several companies in the Chicago area, I was employed by a company called General Finance Corporation. It was a loan conglomerate that dealt in small loans to individuals and in automobile financing to both individuals and to automobile dealers. The automobile end of the business was known both as automobile division and as the "discount" end of the business. The small loan side of the business was just that. Both sides were very well run, the company had an excellent name, and it was one of the leaders in the world of finance.

I worked in the personnel department. My duties, I always felt, were quite interesting, and I enjoyed working under the Personnel Director, Mr. Gordon Goethal. Gordon was a tall handsome fellow with a remarkably cool disposition. There was always good "chemistry" between us, as I understood very plainly the duties he directed me to accomplish. My work-a-day world was, indeed, very pleasant. Gordon's boss was a chap named Al Wonderlic. Al was the Vice President of the Small Loan Division.

Al was also a remarkable fellow. I had heard of him long before I went to work for the company, because Al had developed a personnel test an employer would give to a prospective candidate for a management position in just about any type of industry. It was a unique test with 50 questions involving mostly elementary mathematical problems. The hooker was it had a twelve-minute time limit. Why was it so good? Because it showed how well a person would stand up under pressure.

Al was an excellent administrator. He led the General Finance small loan operation to a level of national respect. He personalized the company with the fictitious name of "Friendly Bob Adams." The company made money under Al Wonderlic.

One of the many duties I had after I had been there a while was to organize and produce the company picnic. I'll tell you—that was a job and a half! But I did it with much help and with considerable delegation. The picnic was a great success. The management was very impressed, because while the picnic was in progress, Gordon and Al both asked me to solve a couple of minor problems that I did by calling upon the people to whom I had assigned certain tasks. My management of the event won high praise from both Gordon and Al. Naturally, as they told me I had done a good job, I said to Al, "Thank you very much, sir."

Immediately he retorted, "Don't call me sir. Call me Al."

"Yessir." I replied. "I mean, okay. I'll call you Al."

Working with Al Wonderlic was not always fun and games. Many times I had to overcome my upbringing.

After all, my dad had brought me up to be respectful of people, and sir and madam were part of that respect. Well, when Al would ask me a question, I'd reply, "Yes sir." Each time, he'd correct me, "Don't call me sir. Call me Al." The more times I made the mistake, the more impatiently came the retort.

Now, my duties as Assistant Personnel Director required that I be responsible for the daily operations of the personnel department. I either designed or simplified many of the procedures for personnel accounting. I handled employee insurance, salesmen's commissions, hiring, and terminations. One day we had a problem. One of the branch managers in a remote city was to be terminated for some infraction he had committed. We were so efficient in our department, that the notice of insurance termination went out about three days too soon.

Al called me into his office to tell me that the branch manager had gotten wind of his termination from the insurance slip. "What happened here, and who did it?" he asked sternly.

"Well, sir," I began. Now he was storming: "GOD DAMMIT DON'T CALL ME SIR! CALL ME AL!!!"

"Well, I have to take the blame for it. Unfortunately it appears our procedure got ahead of us," I explained.

"Who made the mistake?" he pushed. "Did you type out the notice?"

"No, Sir."

"GOD DAMMIT DON'T CALL ME SIR CALL ME AL!!"

So I drew my breath in between my teeth and

continued: "Shirley out at the desk typed the notice, but I really can't blame her. Our procedure just got a little too efficient."

Well, the incident was quickly settled, and I sharpened up our termination notification procedure so it never happened again.

Now, don't be too hard on Al. I learned a very valuable lesson here: a very valuable lesson. Learning to call him Al instead of "sir" was a really good thing. Of course, politeness is also a good thing, but politeness promotes distance and a sterile relationship, business or otherwise. Doing business on a first-name basis taught me to pull closer together with my work associates, and it promoted greater friendliness. After all, when you can call the vice president by his first name, he must think enough of you to consider you part of his inner circle.

I see this same sort of politeness/distance today. Many of us were brought up to "respect" our elders and the people for whom we worked. It's hard to overcome our upbringing, but it's sometimes very fulfilling to get closer to each other to get a more intimate (but not too intimate!) working relationship. Today, people address me as "Mr. Hannas," and I explain to them that "Mr. Hannas was my father, and he left us long ago. I'm Warren."

It wasn't long after that when I learned through my studies of self-esteem and awareness that our most important communications with people are on a subliminal or subconscious level. A first-name relationship is much more fulfilling for me, and it makes a valuable contribution to my self-confidence.

General Finance Corporation was one of my favorite employers, and I left them simply because they moved their offices to one of Chicago's north shore suburbs, and I owned my home in the southwestern suburbs. It was not feasible to live southwest and drive north.

By the way, please remember, if you ever meet me, don't call me sir; call me Warren!

# FOURTEEN

## Here's a Discount for You

WHEN I DEAL WITH PEOPLE ALMOST everywhere I go, I enjoy seeing them smile. Sometimes it lifts someone from a gloomy, run-of-the-mill day to an all new feeling about the day. Sometimes a bit of humor comes back to me which makes my day! Here's a case in point:

Frequently, when paying a bill, I'll ask, "Does this include my 'Good Looking Fellow' Discount?" Believe it or not, there are a myriad of answers that come back:

"It's already figured in."

"Well,...I'll ask the manager about it."

"We don't use that discount here."

"I'll see if we can do that."

"Well, we give discounts for everything else."

"Let me see what we can do."

How would you respond?

But the response I got at a convenience store one day, when I paid for bottle of soft drink, takes the cake. The man behind the counter told me the cost was seventy-five cents. "Do I get a 'Good Looking Fellow' discount?" I asked.

Without a moment's pause, the man looked me squarely in the eye, and said, "Mister, you don't qualify." I'll tell you, that really made my day! I don't know when I have laughed so jubilantly.

# FIFTEEN
## Weasel, My Love

WHEN SHE WAS YOUNG, MY DAUGHTER, Barbara, was a very pretty little girl. Now that she's grown, of course, she's even more beautiful. But in her youth, one of my terms of endearment for her was Weasel. She was, indeed, cute as a weasel, and just as active! She didn't look like a weasel, but, indeed, she was a cutey. Oh, excuse me. Did I say that already? She had blond flaxen hair, and her little blue eyes sparkled vibrantly when she smiled.

My wife and I were always anxious to learn about places in the world other than what we saw every day. We were somehow fortunate enough to have friends in organizations such as the American Field Service Association — or something like that.

On this one occasion, a member of A.F.S. asked us if we'd like to host a gentleman from the Sudan. We thought it was a great idea. Now I know you are familiar with the Sudan, but for those who don't know where it is, it's just south of Egypt in eastern Africa. I can't recall this man's name, but my recollection of him is that he was of medium height, nice appearing, and very friendly. He seemed to be quite well educated, and carried on good conversation. His English was quite good, and he clipped his words as he spoke, which is characteristic of people of that part of the world. He was very dark and had very short hair that resembled an SOS pad. I hate using the word kinky, but that does describe the close-cropped nature of his hair.

As he spoke, he rolled his R's. We might liken it to our making the sound of a running motor: R-r-r-r-r-r. This is easy to do, with the tongue in the front of the mouth, unlike the Germans who roll their R's in their throat. So now, practice rolling your R's, and add the rolling R's to the name Barbara: Bar-r-r-bar-r-r-a.

So on a particular Sunday afternoon, our friend came to have dinner with us. The fellowship was high, and the conversation was active; as he described his country to us, the atmosphere was loving! And he asked questions about our country and about the area where we lived. He described the foods the Sudanese people eat and described in particular a type of tea they drink. All of us were fascinated to learn of each other's surroundings. Cultural exchanges such as this have been a part of my life for many years, and we have often seen how a wonderful understanding of people of far away lands brings us all much closer together.

Also on this occasion, Weasel was four or five years old and was taking in the conversation wide-eyed and all ears. She even asked a question or two of our guest. Soon, the bars of convention broke, and the atmosphere became what we might describe as almost limitless. Our guest, who was sitting next to her turned to her and in a very beautiful way asked, "Bar-r-r-bar-r-a, may I run my hand through your beautiful hair?"

She quickly jumped up in her chair—her own curiosity about to burst and about to be fulfilled—and blurted, "Okay, then I can feel yours!" And she rubbed her hand through his very short black hair. And yes, she did let him run his hand through her soft flaxen hair. Cultural interchange and understanding at its ultimate best! As the visit ended, we were all great friends—even though we have never seen him since.

# SIXTEEN

## The Chili Cook-off

"C'MON, WARREN, ENTER OUR CHILI COOK-OFF on February 18! Everybody has a lot of fun that day."

"The only trouble," I replied, "is that I don't cook chili, and I really don't like my wife's chili."

We had only been members of the church for a couple of months, and, indeed, the congregation had done a marvelous job to welcome us and to make us feel at home. You know, I really wanted to do my part to let them know I wanted to join them in their enterprise. The chili cook-off is one of their many fund raising events of the year, and they wanted me to be a part of it. How could I ever say No?

Well, I'll tell you what I did: I submitted an entry. I thought it would, indeed, be fun to join in the activity of the fundraiser and contribute what little I could to the effort. It only cost $20.00 to submit an entry, and I felt that, in itself, was helping the church.

What would you do in my situation? We had to agree to supply eight quarts of chili, show up with a way to keep it all warm, and serve everyone who chose to buy our chili on the day of the event. I'll tell you what we did: Julie and I went to Kroger's and bought eight jars of Bush's Homestyle Chili. On Saturday morning, Julie got out a huge caldron and cooked the eight jarfuls, while I prepared the two crockpots we used to keep it warm.

We thought it was a very innocuous way to enter the contest where we probably didn't stand a chance of upsetting someone else's winning the contest.

"Contest?" you ask.

You had better believe it! There were two contests. One competition was judged by a panel of well-known, local people: a city alderwoman, a county commissioner, two other people and a representative from the Sheriff's department. The other competition was the popular vote: the chili most of the people who bought the chili liked best. And there were prizes! The judges' contest paid off with a plaque and $50.00. The winner of the popular contest would receive a plaque and a gift certificate to Soprano's, a local restaurant.

Now, there were some guidelines and some rules for the affair: it was against the law to "buy" a vote — that is, buy someone's ticket to get him to vote for your chili. It was against the law to outright pay a person to vote for your chili. It was against the law to try to influence a judge in any way. But there were some enjoyable guidelines, too. For example we could talk to anybody to urge him or her to vote for our chili, and we could, in a sense, electioneer for our offering.

So, at 3:00 o'clock, the doors opened, and people bought tickets to sample the chili being served by all twelve of the contestants. When each person buying a ticket had finished sampling each chili, he or she would deposit his or her ticket into a cup with the number of the chili of his or her choice. The cups were on a table in an adjoining room.

During the afternoon, those in charge of the event took cups full of each member's chili to a back room where the judges sampled and made their selection of the winner. They didn't see the contestants, as each chili sample was numbered.

We felt smug thinking we had no chance to upset the possibilities of those other contestants who had meticulously measured and mixed the ingredients of their distinctive, favorite, homemade chili. After all, our chili was "store-bought" and—so it seemed—not very distinctive.

So I had a ball! Knowing no one would choose our offering, I approached people with what I thought to be a humorous—maybe even silly—worthwhile proposition. "I know that choosing a winner here is a tough job," I would tell them, "but I'll be willing to make the job easy for you. Why don't you just give me your ticket, and I'll do your voting for you." You want to know something? That actually worked once! Yes, one man gave me his ticket and let me do his voting for him.

Well, five o'clock came and the event chairman, Norman, came out to announce the winners. In his hand he held two plaques, a fifty dollar bill, and a gift certificate for the local restaurant. "Here are the winners," he announced happily. "The judges' award of the best tasting chili competition are…(Suspense)…(Suspense)….Julie and Warren Hannas." Applause. Applause. Applause.

"And the winners of the popular vote are . . . Julie and Warren Hannas." More applause.

We weren't applauding. We really don't know if anyone knew that we had bought our chili, but we felt very guilty, because all the others had concocted their own chili, carefully mixing and measuring each ingredient, following a favorite family recipe, and we took the short cut, so to speak. All I can say is I told them at the beginning that I didn't cook, and I didn't like my wife's chili, and I entered anyway. The best I could do was to put the fifty dollar bill in the collection plate in church the next day, and to keep our mixture a secret.

But we did enjoy dinner at Soprano's.

On Wednesday of the next week, I went into the local post office to buy stamps. Our post master—post mistress, actually—greeted me with her usual friendly smile, but for some reason her smile seemed even broader than usual. "Congratulations, Warren."

"Congratulations for what?" I asked.

"For winning the Chili Cook-off. I hear you had really good chili." She was beaming!

"Well," I began, "I'm not sure we should have won the event. It really wasn't our chili. In fact," I continued, "Julie and I feel quite guilty about 'the win.'"

Now she was laughing. "Everyone knows you bought it at the store." she said. "Your minister was just in here, and he told us about it, and someone else had told us about it, too."

Well, we felt better when we learned that almost everybody knew about our purchase.

# SEVENTEEN

## Tolerance Came Easily, But Taught Hard Lessons
*The Race No One Seems to Win*

RACIAL TOLERANCE HAS ALWAYS BEEN a part of my life. It's strange, too, considering my upbringing. My parents were greatly biased people—good folks, make no mistake about that, but they didn't care much for others who were not like them. They held great disdain for foreigners, blacks, Catholics, democrats, Jews. I'm sure there was a reason for all that, and I'm sure the reason was they didn't have the secure, loving, family background that they gave my brothers and me. Indeed, they provided us with a loving secure home.

I never encountered people of other backgrounds until I went to high school. My introduction to black people was extremely good. Nothing out of the ordinary occurred until we were assigned seats for assemblies in the huge high school auditorium. I was assigned a seat next to James Hammock. James was a tall, slender black fellow with features that resembled people I had seen pictured in African stories in the National Geographic magazine.

James was a particularly nice lad, and we got along very well. It wasn't long until I met Paul Smith and his sister, Barbara. Then there was John Pettiford and Sam

Tipton. These, too were really good kids. They all lived in the ghetto of La Grange's east side. We all liked these kids, and got along well. They participated in school activities. I remember John Pettiford was one of the shining stars on the track team. Race was just not a big thing in those days—well, that is, not for me. For them, unfortunately, the picture was quite different. I really didn't know what their feelings were; I just knew there were issues.

I went through college, went to work, climbed a bit as I went from job to job, and finally joined the YMCA and the Y's Men's Club, the service club of the Y. Then I got active in the international organization—Y's Men International, as it later became known. That's when I really became aware of the racial issue. It seemed like the black people in the area almost wanted to declare war on us whites—maybe they did want that! Feelings were certainly high. They had resentment beyond description. I'll tell you; I understood that, and I believed that!

The YMCA and Y's Men International really wanted to do something to ease those tensions, and to make harmonious relations between the races—among all races, in fact. So the two organizations jointly held a seminar on how to get to understanding, primarily between black people and white people. They called a meeting once for a day-long conference. We heard how the blacks disliked many of the racial descriptions—I don't blame them—and they settled on "blacks" and "Afro-Americans" as acceptable. They told how they were discriminated against in the white society, and seemed to be most bitter against discrimination in business. This was largely because promotions seldom went to black people, and there were no blacks at the top management level.

Now I had known some of these black people for a long time, and I liked them very much. I didn't see or feel the business discrimination, as I was an independent businessman, and I wasn't aware of the depth of the resentment and hatred these folks felt. The conversation in the conference was going along well, and I felt they were getting their points across. But I tell you I began to feel frightened, when all of a sudden at the back of the room—B A N G—the rear door flung open, and this enraged black man bolted into the room. As he came down the aisle, he shouted to us white folks, "Enough of this nice talk! You white people don't seem to understand! Your father fucked my mother!"

WOW!!!

At first I was terribly offended. In the first place my dad never did anything like that. Secondly, I didn't think this was the place for such behavior.

But then I began to think. Whether he was right or not, he got our attention. He demonstrated that we're not just talking niceties of folks who were being overlooked for promotions, or who were selectively kept down and kept on the outside in the world. He came through to me just how severely the black people felt, and that we were dealing with deep-seated feelings! We were really going to have to do some real tough understanding and take some real sincere action to bring ourselves closer together. We had a problem!

Now, my membership was in the West Suburban Y's Men's Club in La Grange, Illinois. We decided to meet with the Chatham Y's Men's Club, a black club on the south side of Chicago. We chatted from time to time and found we weren't able to be of any help in securing top-paying jobs for their members, although one of their members was well on the way to top management in Commonwealth Edison Company, Chicago's huge electric utility company.

At one point, one of our members, Bill, a practicing attorney, assured the Chatham men that he did not have racial prejudice. In fact, if any of the Chicago members chose to move next door to Bill, he'd welcome them. Ah, but that wasn't enough.

"Sure," one of them said, "if you really feel that way, then why don't you come down here and move next door to us?" Bill's response was that he believed people should have the right to choose where they want to live. Again, more feelings.

I had a good friend in that Chatham Club named Tanzel Govan. I tell you: I thought the world of Tan. When I became International Director for the Midwest region of Y's Men International, Tan was my Lieutenant International Director, and we made a really good team. At least I thought so. After we served our terms of office, we still kept in touch and visited each other. His wife died soon afterward, and he moved to another part of town, remarried, and I never heard from him after that. His absence is a true void in my life.

We also learned the son of one of the Chatham members was very active in black rights demonstrations. We felt we had to do something to bring the situation into some sort of stability. So, our Y's Men's Club region, which was comprised of clubs in Illinois and Indiana, formed what we called the "Human Crisis Committee" to address the need to unite ourselves and to promote interracial understanding. But as time went on, I began to get the feeling that the particular people we were dealing with really didn't want equality; they wanted superiority. They didn't want to share; they wanted to take over.

As my business progressed, as my independent insurance agency grew, and as I became more active in the community where I lived, racial equality played an ever-decreasing role of importance in my life.

Now, as I am retired, I am living in the south—in beautiful Tennessee, to be exact—and life is altogether different. I live across the street from a church where the congregation is almost 100% black people. My wife, Julie, and I have gotten acquainted with many members of the congregation, and I'm telling you that prejudice just doesn't enter my world. I wish we all could be as loving and as religious as their members and we are. What a much better world we'd have. God bless the members of the Connection Hill Primitive Baptist Church of Thompson's Station, Tennessee! Now, we have attended that church, and we do participate in some of their fundraising activities. We have maintained our membership in our traditional Protestant church, as we have been active there traditionally.

I'm somewhat bothered, however, by the fact that they choose not to participate in community activities. I wouldn't be surprised, though, that sadly, they still don't feel welcome. The bad thing is that every now and then people victimize the church. Racial slurs have been printed on their sign, and one night someone shot holes in their church van. These acts make my blood boil!

So (the) race isn't won, but ultimately, I hope it can be like my world. At least it will be the way I'd like to see people live with one another; in my life color has faded!

Oh, and let me point out one interesting thing: I love reading the Sunday comics. One of my favorite cartoons is "Curtis" drawn by Ray Billingsly. He depicts funny everyday happenings in what I assume to be a typical black family. You know what? The same things happen in typical white families!

# EIGHTEEN

## Frog Legs

ONE TIME I WAS VISITING WITH a friend of mine, having a lively, enthusiastic conversation, when out of the blue—at least so it seamed—he asked me if I had ever eaten frog legs.

"Yes," I said, "I have eaten them. It has been a while, and I really don't remember much about them. I remember that they tasted pretty good, though. Why do you ask?"

"Well," he said, "My wife and I were out to dinner the other night and frog legs were on the menu. I was tempted to get them, but I was afraid I might just start jumping around too much."

"Oh-h-h-h," I told him. "You don't have to worry about that!

He cocked his head to one side and asked quizzically, "Are you sure?"

Well," I said, "I haven't ever been bothered with my legs jumping around after I ate frog legs." And then after a bit of a pause, I explained, "Of course, I have noticed that when a fly walks on the table in front of me, my tongue instinctively reaches out and picks up the fly."

I think I stifled his curiosity for frog legs.

# NINETEEN
## Where'd This Kid Come From, Anyway?

WELL, YOU HAVE COME THIS FAR. I thought maybe—just maybe—you might like to know a little more about me and my family. To me, of course, my roots are important, but you may not think so. Anyway, if you want to get to know me, read on.

I began my journey through life very early in the morning on the sixth day of October in the year 1924. I did not hatch; I was born. This happened at Middlesex County Hospital in New Brunswick, New Jersey. I started out as a lucky little guy, because I had a really great mommy and daddy and a really good older brother. The purpose of my older brother, you know, was to train our parents so that when I came along they had learned from their mistakes from raising him. There are six years between us as he was born November 6, 1918.

I could make this historic chapter easy for me to tell and for you to read by merely saying I was born in the basement and brought up in an elevator. But life isn't that simple, is it?

About two years before I was born, my parents' second child was born. It was a girl, and my mother was thrilled! But six months later, little Harriet Augusta contracted pneumonia, and she died. In a way, we might say that I was the "consolation" for the loss of Harriet, but when I was born, I understand my mother wept with great disappointment, as, of course, I was a little boy.

My father, Ralston Raymond Hannas, was born in 1893, the son of Warren F. Hannas (the one for whom I was named), school teacher—in fact, school principal—and Edith Isabel Cory. My dad grew up where he was born, in Farmingdale, Long Island, New York. He attended Rutgers University in New Brunswick, New Jersey, and earned a Bachelor of Science degree in 1916. Two years later he achieved a masters degree in animal husbandry at Rutgers.

My mother, Leila Aurelia Fisher, was also born in 1893. She was the youngest of seven children born to Thomas Sparks Fisher and Henrietta Williamson. Grandpa Tom was a civil engineer employed by the Pennsylvania Railroad and did a lot of work on the railroad's bridges. The Fisher family was a well-respected family, and it was at a reception held on the campus of Rutgers University that she and Dad met. They were married June 1, 1916. My Aunt Harriet was mother's maid of honor at the wedding. Aunt Harriet was the closest surviving sibling to mother in age. Mother and Aunt Harriet were very close as my brothers and I grew up.

Dad would have loved living on a farm, but mother wanted no part of country livin'. So dad got himself a really nice job as editor of The American Poultry Journal. He held that job for about thirty years or more. Every month he would bring home all the things that were written, and all the illustrations, and all the advertising, and he'd cut and paste and put the magazine together on a card table in the living room! Dad was a good writer, and he had a wonderful sense of humor. All three of us boys either inherited that sense of humor, or we got it by osmosis.

When dad took the job with the journal, we moved to Chicago, where we lived for about a year and a half on south Woodlawn Avenue. In 1927, we moved to Western Springs, Illinois, which is one of Chicago's many lovely suburbs. When we moved to Western Springs, there were just four of us: mom, dad, and my brother, Ralston Junior, and me. Now in those days, I was known as "Brother," a name I sorely detested. We called my brother "Junior" until he went to college. His friends were kinder, though. They called him "Rolly."

I never liked that name: "Brother." In fact I detested it. But I got my mom's attention one day when she had a hard time finding me. It was time for lunch one day, and I heard mother calling me. "Brother!" she called. "BROTHER!" she called again. There was still no answer, so again she called, "B R O T H E R!! Where are you?" There was some anger in her voice, and then she saw me. "I've been calling you! Why didn't you answer?"

"Because my name isn't Brother," I replied with unmistakable indignation. "My name is Warren! And that's my name!" From that day forward, I have been known to everyone as Warren. I have always liked my name: "Warren."

It was about five and a half years after I came into the world that another blessed event occurred. On May

19, 1930, my brother, Allan Everett, was born. I have always felt closer to Allan than to R Square. Allan and I shared many happy moments as we grew up. Allan went to Michigan State University and earned a Bachelor of Science degree in Business. He worked in inventory control for such prestigious companies as Bell and Howell, Ryerson Steel, and Arthur Anderson Company. (It had a good reputation in those days.) Today he and his wife, his high school sweetheart Joan, and I are email buddies. My wife, Julie, isn't quite the computer person I am, so, for Julie, I write all of the emails to Al and Joan.

Mother and dad were both active in the community of Western Springs, Illinois. They attended the Western Springs Congregational church regularly, and they got me in the habit of going to church regularly, and we always attended the family fellowship suppers at the church. Those suppers were such fun! There was always an interesting program, but my strongest memories are of the song leader whose name was John Rowe. John had a resonant bass voice and taught us fun tunes like "Brighten the Corner Where You Are" and "Bar the Door! She's Comin' through the Window" and "Today is Monday" and many others like that. His song leading was intensely enthusiastic. I loved it.

I always felt that I lived in extremely lucky times. Let me tell you why. You see, my dad commuted to and from Chicago by train every day. Many was the time I would ride my bicycle down to the train station at night and walk home with my dad. What I always thought about was the kids who lived in earlier times. Their dads went to work at dawn, and they worked until sun down. So they came home after dark. I'm sure they couldn't have had the family I had. Mother was a homemaker and always had good meals for us. Both dad and mom felt it was necessary for the family to be together for as many meals as possible—and always at supper. Suppertime was almost always family fun time, as you might remember from chapter 3. Today, dads either have to work two jobs or moms also have to get a job to meet family expenses. You see; I lived in the middle of those times. I was truly a very lucky boy.

So anyway, now you can see what sort of family I grew up in. I eally had a nice childhood. My school days were pretty good as I look back on them; I was not the good student R Square was. All he had to do was to look at a book, and he'd get an A+. I had to work hard for all the B's and C's I got, but I've told you more about what happened during my school days in other chapters. I graduated from Lyons Township High School in La Grange, Illinois, in June 1942. I furthered my education at Purdue University in West LaFayette. Indiana. After my first year there, it was time to serve my country, as I was drafted into the military service. (See "World War II Retrospective.") However, after I finished my service in the U. S. Army, I returned to Purdue, and received my bachelor's degree in general science in February 1950. I have been "on the loose" ever since.

During my lifetime, I have had so many fascinating things happen to me, and those are the subjects of the life stories I've decided to share with you throughout this book. I hope you're finding my life to be very entertaining!

One phase of my life for which I seem to have many

a story is my love for trains. How it all started is hard to say. Having observed the progression of my life, and having observed other folks who have a deep interest in trains, I am all but totally convinced that the love for trains comes through the genes. My grandfather and an uncle worked for the Pennsylvania Railroad during the late nineteenth century. As I mentioned earlier, my grandfather Fisher was a civil engineer with the railroad, and he worked on bridges. Gosh, when I drive through Harrisburg, Pennsylvania, I see that long stone arch bridge—I believe it's one of the longest of its type in the country—and I wonder, "Did Grand Daddy have something to do with that?" Then I think, "WOW!"

I don't know what Uncle James did on the railroad. He died young. Thank goodness I haven't followed his example! ...Yet.

When we moved west to the Chicago area, I know it was a big adjustment my mother had to make. When we went to Chicago from Western Springs to shop, we rode the Burlington commuter trains. And before we came home from Chicago, we always went over to the Pennsylvania Railroad side of Union Station. Mother wanted to touch the Broadway Limited, because it was "going home." I kinda think this might also have had an influence on my affinity for the iron pike. Of the three of us sons, R Square and Allan are sports people. I am not. I am the only one of the family with this train thing. Classical music was also bestowed upon me, but not my brothers.

By now you should have a pretty good idea of who I am and how I came to be what I am; anyway, now you know where this kid came from.

# TWENTY

## Big Brother
### Ralston Raymond Hannas, Jr
*(11/06/1918 — 08/06/2005)*

My older brother was born November 6, 1918, in Middlesex Hospital, New Brunswick, New Jersey. He was the first born to Ralston R. Hannas, Sr. and Leila Aurelia Fisher Hannas.

I can't describe what his life was like for his earliest years, as I wasn't around, yet. I can say he taught my parents the art of parenting—a triumph here, and a mistake there, an "Aha!" every now and then, and an "oops" once in a while—so when I came along, they had some pretty good ideas about what was needed to bring up a child, thanks to my big brother.

The early memories I have of this fine gentleman were, of course, when I was small. To begin with, he was known as "Junior." By this time, our family, consisting of our parents and of us two boys, were living in Western Springs, about 15 mile southwest of Chicago.

He taught me a great many things. He taught me how to ice skate, and we skated on Salt Creek not far from our home. On some occasions, we skated from a point nearest home, near Wolf Road and Ogden Avenue, to a bridge over the creek at 31st Street and La Grange

Road. Let me tell you; that was several miles! All the time he reminded me to keep my ankles straight and to keep up with him. Usually one or two of his friends were with us.

Once, he and his friend Gregory Hawk—and I think John Porter was in on this, too—had a potato roast in our back yard. There was a small plot of ground about ten feet square behind our garage, and he and his pals had built a fire and were intending to have a potato roast. But there was one other person who wanted in on this potato roast, but maybe he wasn't old enough. After a great deal of cajoling, my mother finally said it would be all right if Junior said it was okay. I had another sales job on my hands, as you can imagine, but Gregory and John thought it would be okay, so I joined the roast.

Once he had me kinda confused. All of us were assigned things to do around the house on this one day, and his job was washing the windows on the second floor. Our house was built so that this job was not terribly difficult to stand on the roof, which was the overhang for the first floor. Well, Junior told me that tomorrow I'd see a star window washer cleaning the windows. Now, that was very intriguing. What on earth would a star window washer look like? I couldn't picture anything we had that looked like a star. Well, you are probably way ahead of me. The next day the windows were being washed, and who was the star? Of course, Junior was the star; He was the "Star window washer."

He graduated eighth grade from McClure School in Western Springs and went to Lyons Township High School in La Grange. He was smart as a whip. All he had to do was to smell a lesson, and he'd get an A+ in it. He was active in sports. His choice was basketball. One night, he and dad came home from a game he had played in, and they were so keyed up, it seemed it took them an hour to calm down. Junior had made the winning basket, and La Grange won the game! Truly, Junior got a very good start in life. He was a really good boy, and a wonderful brother.

He chose to attend Purdue University to further his schooling. He selected the science course, because he set his sights on becoming a doctor. Now Purdue was considered a top-flight school in engineering as well as science and agriculture. This is necessary to know, because he was bound and determined to shake off that name: "Junior." And who could blame him? He learned that when you multiply a number by itself, it was known as "squaring it." Since his initials were "R R " it constituted R Square. Consequently he was known forever after as "R Square" Hannas.

Now, he was as brilliant in college as he was in high school. His grades were top notch. There was something new at Purdue, though, that he hadn't encountered previously. Since Purdue University was a land grant college, R.O.T.C. (Rear Officers Training Corps) was a mandatory part of the curriculum. During his time at college, he took to this R.O.T.C. like a duck to water, and during his senior year, he had earned the title "Cadet Colonel." Yeah. He was "Top Da-a-w-wg!" Our family made a special trip to Purdue toward the end of his senior year to see him lead all of the members of the corps as Cadet Colonel. Believe me — that was quite a show!

When he graduated, he enlisted in the United States Marine Corps as a second Lieutenant. He served during World War II in Camp Lejune, North Carolina, finally ending up as a major on the Island of American Samoa. Here, he contracted a tropical disease known as Elephantiasis. He was sent to Great Lakes, Illinois, for treatment, where he responded well and healed completely.

He married Lucy Demoret whom he had met in college, and they produced six lovely children, one of whom died at an early age from Leukemia.

His medical career flourished, and in the middle 1970s he became one of the founders of the American College of Emergency Room Physicians. He was, indeed, skilled at operating and managing a hospital emergency room. He was known nation-wide for his accomplishments.

His marriage with Lucy dissolved, and he married a nurse with whom he had worked in an emergency room in Kansas City, Missouri. Kay Johnson was his partner, his soul mate, and best friend. The marriage was as close to ideal as it could be; however, she passed away in February 1993.

He finally retired to Tucson, Arizona, and in August 2005, he surrendered his trophies to the Lord as the result of a malignant brain tumor.

Quite a guy!

# TWENTY-ONE

## Allan

ALLAN IS MY YOUNGER BROTHER. It was easy to describe my older brother as "Big Brother," but it's difficult to describe Allan as my "Little Brother." He's the baby. But, God forbid, I'd never say that! After all, he may be younger, but he's a bit taller than I am, so "Little Brother" doesn't fit. Younger brother? Well, okay, but that tends to destroy the equality of life that Al and I shared as youngsters at home.

Allan Everett Hannas was born on May 19, 1930, in Hinsdale, Illinois. My poor mom bore him alone, because dad was on a trip to Europe in connection with his job as editor of the American Poultry Journal. And, as it happened, even I wasn't home. However, at age 5 ½, I wouldn't have been any help at all, anyway. I was in New Jersey visiting Aunt Harriet, and waiting for dad to return from Europe so that I could ride the train home with him from New York City. It was also the first time I had met my paternal grandmother.

During his way up the school ladder, "Junior," as R Square was then known, went on to Purdue and wasn't home much any more. I felt a very warm closeness with

Allan. I just know I wasn't the good teaching brother that "Junior" had been for me, but Allan and I seemed to have fun together.

I can remember one cold, snowy day in our driveway: Al and I were shoveling snow, when we were attacked by snowballs by a couple of boys from our neighborhood—friends of ours, of course. Al and I quickly amalgamated into a pretty effective team, and we drove off the "enemy" in short order.

When I came home from army service, I experienced one of the greatest train rides of my life. Having left Rockford, Illinois, 2 ½ hours late, the train arrived at Union Station right on time. The distance was ninety miles! There to greet me were my dad and my brother, Al! What a great welcoming party they were—the perfect end to a train ride that was incomparably fast, and one that was bringing me home to close an important chapter in my life!

Now, if I recall correctly, I don't think Al had graduated from high school yet, so dad took me aside one day, and very nicely asked me not to share my army jokes with Al, because he was still quite young and impressionable. Al, on the other hand, took me aside one day, and very nicely told me some of the jokes he and his high school friends had shared. I tell you; I was very careful not to pollute my dad's ears.

I think Al got better grades in high school than I did, but then I'm not really sure. When he graduated from high school, Al chose to study business administration at Michigan State University. He was also active in gymnastics there. His specialty was trampoline performance.

I will never forget an intercollegiate gymnastic performance between Michigan State University and the University of Illinois at the University of Illinois Navy Pier campus one very cold evening. Things had gone well—at least for Al—but for me it was kind of boring until one young man competed on the flying rings. Up and down, changing positions, and all sorts of maneuvers this chap did! It was quite a routine until he reached the top of one action. Now, imagine this: high in the gym, a young man on the rings, his arms straight as arrows, and his body bent in the middle. The place was so quiet that you could hear a pin drop! All of a sudden came the unmistakable sound of a healthy attack of flatulence. First it was quiet. . . dead silence. . . then one or two people began to titter. . . then others giggled, and finally, the entire population broke out in uproarious laughter! The poor fellow must have felt like a penny waiting for change! He must have felt much embarrassment.

Well, when Al finished college, he married his high school sweetheart, Joan Van de Houten. Joan and Al are still married to each other today, sharing and enjoying a happy life of retirement, but I'll tell you more about that later.

After Al finished college and his army service requirement, he began work in inventory control with Bell and Howell Company. To be close to his work, he and Joan rented an apartment in Rogers Park on Chicago's north side. Apartments were scarce, so they signed a lease where they would buy the electrical fixtures for the apartment. After a short time, it became apparent that the fixtures must be purchased from the landlord's son at the son's electrical outlet store. (The landlord, himself, was a practicing dentist.) The idea of this scheme went like this: you buy fixtures for the apartment—after you move, fixtures are returned to son's store. Al wanted none of that scheme, so he then decided to break his lease. He asked the Bell and Howell Corporate Council to prepare a release document that he could use to get out from under that lease, which they did. This document was to be hand-delivered to the dentist landlord at the dentist's office. Al called me to ask if I would join him when he delivered the release document. I was to be a witness to whatever would happen. The way things turned out, I wore a dark blue pin stripe suit and carried a professional looking brief case. I presented the papers to the landlord. Now, the humor in this episode is that when the landlord saw me looking like an attorney with my brief case and my demeanor as "representing" my client (Brother Al), he just melted like a dish of ice cream. Apologetically, and with a broad grin, he signed the papers willingly, and the case was closed! Our motto: "Don't tread on us."

Joan and Al have five great, successful kids who are fun to be around. But all too soon, the family moved from Illinois to Summit, New Jersey, and ultimately to northern New Jersey where they are now retired. Al and Joan are professionals. Al has a woodworking and metal shop that he uses to turn out incredible home projects, and Joan is a master gardener. She starts gardening in their basement in the wintertime, raising masterful flowers and vegetables for transplanting into their summer gardens.

Great folks!

# TWENTY-TWO

## Aunt Harriet

AUNT HARRIET WAS MY MOTHER'S SISTER. for most of the years I knew them, they were quite close. They had grown up together. There were three of them who were close in age and therefore in spirit. Their father was Thomas Sparks Fisher, and their mother was Henrietta Augusta Williamson. They had seven children: Mary Eliza, William Williamson, Charles Edward, Alice Cogswell, Harriet Mott, James Henry, and Leila Aurelia. Leila was my mother. William and Alice did not live long. Grandfather Thomas Fisher was a civil engineer with the Pennsylvania Railroad and worked on bridges. James Henry grew to maturity, and I believe went to work for the Pennsylvania Railroad. One fine bright, sunny Sunday, however, James went canoeing on the Raritan River and got horribly sunburnt, developed pneumonia, and died as a result.

Harriet, James, and Leila were the three youngest, and were closest together. Now, since James had passed away, sisters Harriet and Leila became fast-friends as well. Harriet was my mother's maid of honor at mother's marriage to my father, Ralston R. Hannas. Aunt Harriet never married.

I always wondered why Aunt Harriet never married. She was a very intelligent woman with an educated background, having graduated from what is now the New Jersey State Teachers College. I believe it is part of Rutgers University. For almost as long as I knew her, she had been principal of Hamilton Elementary School in Highland Park, New Jersey. Highland Park was just east across the Raritan River from New Brunswick where the Fisher "clan" was deeply rooted. Later in my life I learned that she had been deeply in love with a man whom she had been actively dating. She was planning to marry him, but when the push came to a shove, she learned that he was already married! This devastated her, and she never trusted a man again.

In 1927, after my parents had been married for about eleven years, dad took a job in Chicago and moved all of us west from Highland Park, New Jersey, to Chicago. By that time my older brother was nine years old, and I was not quite three. It separated mother and Aunt Harriet for the first time, and it must have been difficult for both of them. But the nice thing was that Aunt Harriet came out to visit us twice a year. We always looked forward to Aunt Harriet's visits. As early as I can recall, she drove her car out to our home in Western Springs, Illinois, in the summertime and came out on the train at Christmastime. We used to go into Chicago Union Station to watch for the headlight of her train to appear at the end of the station and then anticipate its dramatic easing to a stop. Then we waited for Aunt Harriet to come up the platform. It was exciting, indeed!

Frequently, when she drove out in the summer, we

would go on trips. I can remember one trip in particular when I was about twelve years old. We drove out to Colorado. My Aunt Harriet did all the driving, because my parents didn't own a car, and they didn't know how to drive. We all had a wonderful time. My dad, mother, my brother Allan, and I all enjoyed seeing Denver, Colorado Springs, and some of the front range of the Rockies. There were two times when I thought my mother would die of fright: the first of those times was our venture up Pikes Peak. Aunt Harriet's car did very well climbing up, and we enjoyed the incomparable sights from that elevation, even though we almost froze! But going down the mountain was hair-raising! Mother would look over the side of the road with great fear. If the car didn't go off the road, she was afraid the road would collapse. Believe me. The road to Pikes Peak today, although still not paved all the way, is a far cry from what it was in 1936!

The second Colorado adventure took us southwest of Colorado Springs, to Cripple Creek. On the way back to major roads, we traveled on a dirt road that led to a very rickety bridge. I can't recall exactly how we were told of the dangerous condition of the bridge, but when we reached it, it was, indeed, a hazard. In fact, Aunt Harriet herself suggested we walk across the bridge so she could drive just the car across with that much less weight. All of the rest of us walked across, and turned around to watch Aunt Harriet drive across this perilous structure. Our hearts were in our throats as we drew a deep breath and watched the car inch over the timbers of this threatening, old span.

Whew! She finally made it! With gladdened hearts,

we climbed back into the car and drove back to Denver where we had been staying at a motel. The trip home was uneventful.

Among the many things I learned from Aunt Harriet, she taught me how to read a map. Now one of the talents God has given me was an almost infallible sense of direction. I have often wondered whether it came from my aunt's teaching me how to read maps, or whether it's in my genetic make-up. But I have always credited Aunt Harriet for her teaching me that skill.

Manners were always important to her. One of my strongest memories is when she would very discreetly lean toward us and quietly tell us, "Take your elbows off the table, Honey Dear." But as we grew older the admonition grew more and more obnoxious.

Her late and waning years were pitiful, as is the case with many older folks who had been pinnacles of honor in their early years. It became necessary for my younger brother, Allan, to care for Aunt Harriet and to take on the chaotic state of affairs of her estate.

If we were to add up her good points and subtract her less attractive attributes, she was a wonderful lady!

---

Fisher, Philip A, THE FISHER GENEALOGY, Page 385, No.837, Pub 1898, Massachusetts Publishing Company. Everett, Mass.

# TWENTY-THREE

## AT THE END OF THE MEAL: DESSERT

WELL, I HOPE YOU HAVE ENJOYED READING the stories of my life. I hope you had some good laughs, and I hope I gave you some things to think about. Now it's time for the good stuff. I want to tell you about my partner, my best friend, my soul mate—my wife, Julie. Julie is my second wife: this is the second marriage for both of us. It's the marriage that isn't supposed to last. Right now, as I prepare to publish these stories, we have celebrated more than forty-one happy years together.

Between us we have seven children. She had five in her first marriage, and I had two in mine. In order of their ages from eldest to youngest, they are Robert, George, Pamela, Jeannette, Carol, Barbara, and Stuart. Robert owns a plumbing company; Doctor George, Ed.D., is a curriculum specialist and a college professor; Pamela is a letter carrying specialist; Jeannette is a physical therapist; Carol is a hospital nurse; Barbara is an independent community nurse; and Stuart is a computer program specialist. At this point they are all doing well, and we pride ourselves on being a cohesive family of nine folks.

So how did we meet? While I started my insurance business, I drove a taxi in Hinsdale, Illinois. Ultimately the owner of the taxi company was Julie's first husband, Dunbar (Cub) Bair. Bob, the eldest son, bought a car and needed automobile insurance. They asked me to obtain insurance for him, which I did. After a few months, Julie, Bob's mother, called me to tell me she needed auto insurance, too. So I got her insured. Now in the meantime, she and Cub split and divorced.

Now that's all fine, but the divorce left Julie very short of money. (I should have been a lawyer instead of an insurance man!) She had trouble keeping up her payments to the insurance man—me. Well, it looked like if I were going to have her insurance paid, I was going to have to marry her.

Well, of course, there was a lot more to it than that. She and her mother and the girls often invited me for Sunday dinner. Being a divorced man, myself, I accepted the invitations with glee. Now, I have always been one to "tell it like it is," so to speak, and when I would give one of my opinions on something, Nana, who we all knew better as Julie's mother, would turn to Julie and say, "Julia, who does that sound like?"

Always the answer came back, "It sounds like something dad would say."

I figured that if I think a lot like her dad, it was a good thing. (Good heavenly days! Was there someone else like me in the world?) Her dad, Mr. Harry Carroll, had passed away 20 years before I showed up. If we were to marry, the marriage would probably be quite compatible. So on another occasion, at the dining room table, with her two youngest daughters and her mother present, I asked Julie to marry me. Would you believe? She said yes! The wedding was scheduled for February 25th after a record snowfall, and the family members who were able to be there were involved in the wedding, and a new family was launched. Many folks who knew me predicted the marriage would probably not even last six months. Let's see: how many months are there in forty-one years? I'd say it has been a pretty successful love affair. Wouldn't you?

Julie is loved by everyone who knows her. She always has an encouraging word for other people. And what a joy she is to me!

Through the years we have enjoyed each other's interests, we have kept humor as a very active part of our marriage, and almost everything we do, we do together. We attended model train club meetings together, we went to doll shows together, we always travel together, and church is an activity both of us share actively. Julie is known in our town as a storyteller. She tells stories to children in a day care center and to children at the library. We both serve on the board of directors of the Friends of the Spring Hill Library. I serve as Lay Leader at our Thompson's Station United Methodist Church, and I am a certified lay speaker occasionally asked to give the sermon at church.

Our lives are full, we keep busy, and we are always interested in new things. All these elements are the glue that has kept us happily together, and we expect it will continue to do that for a long time to come!

May God bless all of you and keep you, and may His face shine upon you. May He be before you to lead, behind you to push, beside you to comfort you, and above you to smile upon you. Keep mindful of the gifts and talents God has given you, and may He keep you safe, always.

CPSIA information can be obtained at www.ICGtesting.com
Printed in the USA
245421LV00001BA/61/P